Distress Tolerance Made Easy

Dialectical Behavior Therapy Skills For Dealing With Intense Emotions In Difficult Times

Sheri Van Dijk, MSW, • Matthew McKay, PhD
Jeffrey C. Wood, PsyD, • Jeffrey Brantley, MD
• Patrick Fanning
Erica Pool, PsyD • Patricia E. Zurita Ona, PsyD

16pt

Copyright Page from the Original Book

Publisher's Note

This publication is designed to provide accurate and authoritative information in regard to the subject matter covered. It is sold with the understanding that the publisher is not engaged in rendering psychological, financial, legal, or other professional services. If expert assistance or counseling is needed, the services of a competent professional should be sought.

NEW HARBINGER PUBLICATIONS is a registered trademark of New Harbinger Publications, Inc.

New Harbinger Publications is an employee-owned company.

Copyright © 2023 by Sheri Van Dijk, Matthew McKay, Jeffrey C. Wood, Jeffrey Brantley, Patrick Fanning, Erica Pool, and Patricia E. Zurita Ona
New Harbinger Publications, Inc.
5720 Shattuck Avenue
Oakland, CA 94609
www.newharbinger.com

All Rights Reserved

Cover design by Amy Daniel; Interior Design by Michele Waters-Kermes; Acquired by Georgia Kolias; Edited by Joyce Wu

---

Library of Congress Cataloging-in-Publication Data on file

TABLE OF CONTENTS

Introduction: WHY DISTRESS TOLERANCE?	iii
Chapter 1: LEARN YOUR EMOTIONAL LANDSCAPE	1
Chapter 2: PAUSE AND OBSERVE	28
Chapter 3: SOOTHE AND CALM USING YOUR SENSES AND BODY	50
Chapter 4: BE KIND TO YOURSELF	67
Chapter 5: TAKE REFUGE FROM YOUR PAIN	76
Chapter 6: ACCEPT AND MOVE BEYOND	108
CONCLUSION	129
REFERENCES	132
BACK COVER MATERIAL	141

"As a fellow dialectical behavior therapy (DBT) therapist, author, and trainer, I am always on the lookout for simple, practical, and effective ways of making DBT skills accessible to the average reader. In this book, you will find just that! Even after using, teaching, and writing about DBT concepts for more than a decade, I now have a richer understanding of distress tolerance that I am excited to try on myself—and share with others!"

—**Kirby Reutter, PhD,** bilingual clinical psychologist with the Department of Homeland Security, and author of *The Dialectical Behavior Therapy Skills Workbook for PTSD*

"For those looking for practical and accessible distress tolerance skills, this book is for you. *Distress Tolerance Made Easy* compiles a list of simple and must-have coping strategies to add to your repertoire. With guidance and scripts, this book will lead you to finding the skills that suit you best during moments of distress. You're guaranteed to walk away with several tools to help you face strong emotions."

—**Dylan Zambrano, MSW,** founder of DBT Virtual, and author of *The DBT Skills Daily Journal*

"People who struggle with intense emotions and self-destructive behavior will benefit from the information in this book. The authors have done an excellent job of teaching skills that are simple, clear, accessible, and true to DBT. Valuable for adults and adolescents!"

—**Cedar Koons, LCSW,** author of *The Mindfulness Solution for Intense Emotions*

"*Distress Tolerance Made Easy* is an excellent resource for anyone wanting an in-depth look at some of the most valuable skills DBT has to offer. This book offers readers a deeper understanding of what our emotions do for us, and what it means to ride the wave of your emotions without letting them overtake you. These vitally important skills are offered in a way that is compassionate, and easy to understand and practice."

—**Emma Lauer, LCSW,** author of *DBT Skills for Highly Sensitive People*

"A much-needed, valuable guide to making sense of distress—and responding more effectively to it. This empowering resource will help you decide when to act on emotions, work through them to prioritize meaningful action, or practice self-compassionate acceptance."

—**Joel Minden, PhD,** clinical psychologist, and author of *Show Your Anxiety Who's Boss*

Introduction

WHY DISTRESS TOLERANCE?

We all get dysregulated sometimes—when our emotions get intense and we feel overwhelmed as a result. Of course, this looks different for everyone—for some, it might feel like shutting down, stuffing emotions, or perhaps isolating ourselves from others, physically or just emotionally. For others, it may mean feeling out of control, ruminating, and venting frustration. And for still others, it may come out in very unhealthy behaviors such as lashing out at people, or lashing out at themselves in the form of self-judgment and blaming, or even self-harm or suicidal thoughts or behaviors.

Whatever intense emotion looks like for you right now, it's important to know that part of learning to manage emotions more effectively is learning to tolerate distress. But what does *learning to tolerate distress* mean, exactly? Distress tolerance involves being able to tolerate emotional distress so you can get through difficult experiences in ways that don't result in negative consequences. Many people learn skills to manage their emotions as they grow up, and as a result, regulating emotions becomes a natural process. But there are times when things get especially distressing and we have to consciously put more effort into this process. And of course, some people never learned healthy ways of managing emotions in the first place.

Regardless of which category you fall into—whether you have skills that you would like to enhance to improve your life, you never learned these skills at all, or you fall somewhere in between—the goal of this book is to teach a variety of skills and provide practical exercises that will help you improve your capabilities and your confidence in your abilities to tolerate distress. The skills you'll find in this book will help you get through crisis situations without making things worse by falling back on problematic behaviors you may have used in the past; and you'll find fast-acting, effective, and scientifically proven strategies that will help you stop making problematic choices in the moments when your emotions are overwhelming you.

What Is Dialectical Behavior Therapy?

The skills in this book are based on a psychological treatment called *dialectical behavior therapy* (DBT), created by Dr. Marsha Linehan. She developed DBT to treat people with borderline personality disorder (BPD), an illness of which one of the main components is emotion dysregulation. Since its creation, however, countless studies have shown how effective DBT is in helping people regulate their emotions in healthier ways, even when they don't have a diagnosis of BPD. The fact is, DBT is a wonderfully helpful therapy that teaches us skills to manage emotions more effectively—including learning to tolerate distress. And since life doesn't always go as smoothly as we would like, we all need skills like these at times.

Instructions for Using This Book

Keep in mind that simply reading a book like this typically isn't going to help you make meaningful changes in your life. What will help you to really learn the skills is to read about each skill, follow the instructions to practice them, and then practice the skills regularly to build your proficiency with them. There are two specific things that will be important for you to know.

First, it is very important to personalize the skills you'll be reading about—making them your own to increase the chances you'll use them as well as to enhance their efficacy. Since everyone is different and experiences emotional distress differently, it's important that these skills make sense for you. To help remind you of the skills you've learned and start integrating them into your life, we recommend you keep a dedicated journal as you work through the book. In the journal or notebook, you can keep a list of skills you learn and respond to the prompts and exercises.

Second, some of the skills you'll be learning will involve engaging in formal, scripted exercises, where you'll be asked to set aside a specific amount of time to sit quietly and turn inward in some way. For these practices, you'll have some options:
- You can read through the script a couple of times until you have the feel of it, and then start the practice.
- You might want to read through the script as you do the practice; or you can also have someone else read it to you as you practice, if that's comfortable for you.
- You may choose to record yourself or someone else reading the script (for example, on your smartphone), and then you can listen to the recording as you do the practice.

You might want to experiment with each of these methods to see what works best for you. Whatever you choose, be sure you set aside some quiet time to do these practices, when you'll likely be undisturbed, so you can really turn your attention and energy to the exercise. You might notice that the exercises themselves and turning your attention inward can sometimes bring up distress, in which case you can turn to some of the other skills you'll be learning to help you tolerate that discomfort!

We're confident that this compilation of skills will be helpful, and we hope you enjoy them!

Chapter 1

LEARN YOUR EMOTIONAL LANDSCAPE

It's actually quite common for people to not recognize the emotions they're experiencing. In the extreme, some people struggle to feel and put words to any emotion; whereas others may only be able to identify some of the emotions they experience. If this is you, you might find yourself walking around in an emotional fog, not aware of the feelings you're having, or aware that you feel *bad* or *upset*, but not being able to put an accurate label on the emotion. This can lead to problems as emotions take over and cause some people to act in ways that have negative consequences (like lashing out at others). But even if that's not the case for you, naming emotions accurately is an important skill to have. In order to tame emotions, we must be able to name them (Siegel 2014); this is why you need to get to know your emotions better. To help with this, we'll be taking a closer look at some of the basic human emotions, their purpose, and information and strategies to help you accurately identify and label them, including exercises to help you unravel their different components.

What Is an Emotion?

Although we often refer to emotions as "feelings," the feeling aspect is just one part of the experience. Emotions are, in fact, *full system responses* that involve thoughts, physical sensations, urges, and behaviors (Linehan 1993). Because there's so much going on when we're feeling an emotion, it can be difficult to tell the difference between how we *feel*, what we *think* (the thoughts), and what we *do* (the behaviors). For example, if you're experiencing the emotion of curiosity, you're going to *feel* curious, which would include physical sensations in your body (like tilting your head to the side, raised eyebrows, and body language that perks up). Your *thought* might be, *I'm curious about what this book has to offer about managing my emotions in more effective ways!* And the *behavior* might be to continue reading. *Urges*, by the way, are a combination of emotions and thoughts. In the previous example, for instance, the urge would be a combination of the *emotion* of curiosity and the *thought* of continuing to read, both of which precede the action.

Naming Emotions

Researchers still disagree about which emotions are "basic" human emotions—those that are universal experiences and are hardwired into us. In DBT, ten basic emotions have been identified: anger, fear, sadness, guilt, shame, envy, jealousy, disgust, love, and happiness (Linehan 2014). We won't be offering an in-depth analysis of all of these emotions, just the ones that most commonly contribute to emotion dysregulation. So, keep in mind that if you finish this chapter and still have questions about some of the emotions that cause you difficulties, you may need to do more work in this area outside of what's offered here. For some people, happiness, love, and other pleasurable emotions are problematic (for instance, some people might engage in impulsive behaviors when they're feeling happiness or love, whereas others might have beliefs like they're not deserving of these emotions). Please keep in mind that you can use the skills in this book to help you manage even the more pleasurable emotions.

What You Need to Know About Emotions

From a DBT perspective, every emotion serves a purpose or can be *justified* at times, meaning that they make sense given the situation.

In the following pages (adapted from Linehan 2014), you'll learn about the function of some of the more common painful emotions; the urges, thoughts, and body sensations associated with each; and different words for each. You'll also have an opportunity to consider your own experience of these emotions, since everyone experiences emotions differently.

You're not expected to remember all of the following information. Rather, when you experience an emotion, you'll want to refer back to these pages so you gradually learn how to name your emotions accurately (or confirm that you're already labeling them accurately). We suggest that you thoroughly read about these emotions now, and come back to them periodically to help you complete the self-inquiry exercises provided later in this chapter. Keep your journal handy so you can respond to the self-inquiry sections to dig a little deeper into your personal experience with each emotion.

Anger

Anger's purpose. Anger arises when someone or something is getting in the way of you moving toward a goal, or when you or someone you care about is being attacked, threatened, insulted, or hurt by others.

What anger does. Anger typically causes people to become aggressive, possibly causing them to physically or verbally attack what they see as dangerous, to make the threat go away. When the human race was evolving and there were constant threats in the environment, anger helped us survive.

Example of when anger is justified. You get passed over for a promotion even though you have seniority and your performance appraisals have been good. Your boss has prevented you from reaching a goal, so it makes sense and is justified that you feel angry in this situation.

Examples of anger thoughts. *This is ridiculous. They can't get away with this; that promotion should have been mine. They don't know what they're doing.* Usually anger thoughts involve judgments (like *This is ridiculous*), thinking what's happening shouldn't be happening or that people shouldn't be the way they are.

Body sensations:

Tense or tight muscles, such as clenching fists or jaw (your body preparing you to fight in a dangerous situation)

Trembling or shaking

Racing heart

Increased breathing rate

Change in body temperature, which might lead to feeling hot or cold

Urges and behavior. Anger usually involves aggression, so you might yell, scream, swear, or say hurtful things to someone, or you might even physically lash out, throw things, or hit or punch things or people (including yourself). It's important to note that just because a feeling is justified, it doesn't mean you should act on the urges associated with it. For example, you can feel anger at your boss for not giving you what you want and choose not to respond to your urge to quit your job or verbally abuse your boss.

Other words for feeling anger:
Annoyed
Exasperated
Mad
Aggravated
Cross
Outraged
Indignant
Frustrated
Resentful
Irate
Bothered
Impatient
Hostile
Irritated
Bitter
Furious
Incensed
Enraged
Peeved

Self-Inquiry: Anger
Think of a recent time when you felt angry, and describe the situation. What happened? What urges did you notice when

you were in the situation you described? What did you actually do? Can you think of other words that fit better to describe what you experienced?

Fear and Anxiety

Fear is different from but very related to anxiety. Fear and anxiety essentially feel the same physically. The main difference between them is that fear is present focused and related to a specific threat; it motivates you to act by triggering the fight-or-flight response, which helps you survive in dangerous situations. Anxiety, however, comes up when there's a more general threat you're worrying about—something that hasn't happened yet and may never happen. It also comes up when there's something you might reasonably expect to happen and you expect the results to be catastrophic, or out of proportion with reality. So, if you're driving on the highway and you're thinking *What if someone hits me?* you're likely going to feel anxious.

While there are definitely times when fear is justified, there is rarely a time when you *should* feel anxious, or when you can say that your anxiety would be justified, because anxiety involves a fear of something that isn't a real or immediate threat—even if it feels that way! Some anxiety is helpful, because without it you wouldn't be cautious while you're driving, which might make you less likely to leave enough space between you and the car ahead of you. Without some anxiety, you might take more risks, like driving too fast. So we're not trying to get rid of anxiety (or any emotion, for that matter, since all emotions serve a purpose), but if you have anxiety regularly—or to the extreme, such as by having panic attacks—you want to be able to manage it better, instead of letting it control you.

Fear's purpose. Fear comes up when there's a danger to your health, your safety, or your well-being or to that of someone you care about.

What fear does. Fear motivates you to act to protect yourself or those you care about.

Example of when fear is justified. You're driving down a busy freeway at seventy miles per hour and you see traffic coming to a dead stop not far in front of you. Fear is justified because your safety is threatened.

Examples of anxiety thoughts. Anxious thoughts are future-focused catastrophizing or worry thoughts often consisting of *what-ifs*: What if I make a fool of myself? What if I can't do it? What if that car hits me?

Body sensations:
- Tense or tight muscles (your body preparing you to flee a dangerous situation)
- Trembling or shaking muscles
- Racing heart
- Increased breathing rate
- Change in body temperature, which might lead to feeling hot or cold

Urges and behaviors. With fear, urges and behaviors usually involve running away from the threat to protect yourself or the people you care about. With anxiety, urges and behaviors usually involve avoiding a situation (like choosing not to go to work because you're worried that you'll have a panic attack and make a fool of yourself) or escaping the situation if you're already in it (like leaving work early, because you're feeling anxious).

Other words for feeling fear:
Trepidation
Scared
Worried
Stressed
Edgy
Troubled
Uneasy
Panicky
Apprehensive
Dread
Startled
Jumpy
Anxious
Terrified
Nervous
Disturbed
Alarmed
Jittery
Concerned

Self-Inquiry: Fear and Anxiety

Think of a recent time when you felt fearful or anxious, and describe the situation. What happened? What urges did you notice when you were in the situation you described? What did you actually do? Can you think of other words that fit better to describe what you experienced?

As you recalled your experience of fear or anxiety, did you notice a similarity to what you experience when you feel angry? The body sensations can be very much the same, which is one reason why it can be easy to mix up feelings of fear or anxiety and anger!

Sadness

Sadness's purpose. Sadness is the emotion felt when things aren't the way you expected them to be or when you've experienced a loss of some sort.

What sadness does. This is the emotion that encourages people around you to try to be of help or to offer support. It might also motivate you to try to regain what you've lost, or to seek comfort from others.

Examples of when sadness is justified. You didn't get a job you really wanted, your partner is ending your relationship, or someone close to you receives a diagnosis of a terminal illness. Sadness is justified in these situations because you've experienced loss, and because things aren't as you had expected them to be.

Examples of sadness thoughts. When we're feeling sad, our tendency is to focus on the loss we've experienced and on the disappointment we feel. Some examples of sadness thoughts include *Things are hopeless, I'm not worthwhile, I'm unloved,* or *I have no one.*

Body sensations:
Tightness in chest or throat

Heaviness in chest or heart

Tears in eyes

Slumped posture

Tired or heavy body

Urges and behaviors. Urges and behaviors associated with feeling sad often involve withdrawing from others, isolating ourselves, or crying.

Other words for feeling sadness:
Disappointed
Resigned
Despair
Anguish
Depressed
Downhearted
Discouraged

Hopeless
Grief
Down
Heartbroken
Unhappy
Distraught
Miserable
Sorrow
Distressed
Glum
Despondent

Self-Inquiry: Sadness

Think of a recent time when you felt sad, and describe the situation. What happened? What urges did you notice when you were in the situation you described? What did you actually do? Can you think of other words that fit better to describe what you experienced?

Guilt

We often feel guilt and shame in the same situations, and many aspects of these emotions are similar, which can cause us to confuse them. These two emotions are very common for people who experience emotion dysregulation, and shame especially can be very powerful in keeping people dysregulated. We'll cover shame next.

Guilt's purpose. Guilt is the feeling that comes up when you've done something that goes against your values and you judge your behavior.

What guilt does. Guilt motivates you to make amends and prevents you from acting a certain way in the future.

Examples of when guilt is justified. You say something to purposely hurt your partner during an argument, or your boss overpays you and you decide to keep the money and not tell them. Your behavior in both situations doesn't match your values, so you feel guilty.

Examples of guilt thoughts. When feeling guilty, we tend to think judgmental thoughts about our behavior: *That was wrong, I shouldn't have done that. If only I had done things differently. It's my fault.* We might also dwell on past behaviors when feeling guilty.

Body sensations:

Feeling jittery or agitated

Hot, flushed face

Bowed head

Urges and behaviors. When feeling guilty, you often want to make amends (apologizing to your partner, for example) to try to make up for what you did.

Other words for feeling guilt:
Remorseful

Regretful
Contrition
Apologetic
Self-reproach
Sorry

Self-Inquiry: Guilt

Think of a recent time when you felt guilt, and describe the situation. What happened? What urges did you notice when you were in the situation you described? What did you actually do? Can you think of other words that fit better to describe what you experienced?

Shame

Shame's purpose. Shame protects you by keeping you connected to others. Shame arises when you've done something, or when there is something about you as a person, that you fear might cause people to reject you if they knew about it. Part of this involves self-judgment, where you judge yourself for this thing, and you anticipate that others will also judge you.

What shame does. Shame causes you to hide—your behavior, or that characteristic of yourself—so you can remain connected to people who are important to you. Shame is also the emotion that comes up to stop you from doing that same behavior again in future. If people know about your behavior (or characteristic), shame causes you to try to make amends in those relationships.

Examples of when shame is justified. You engage in a behavior like drinking, using drugs, or gambling as a means of dealing with your emotions, and you hide your behavior so others won't reject you for it. Whether shame is justified in this example depends on whom you're hiding from. Some people might reject you for what you did, in which case shame is justified; it's causing you to hide the behavior, protecting you by keeping you connected. But others (like your significant other, your best friend, or your therapist) hopefully would not reject you, in which case shame would not be justified. Shame is also justified if you cheat on your partner, because quite possibly they will reject you if they find out, and shame is there to stop you from doing the same behavior again in future.

You may also experience shame if there's something that makes you different from others, or at least you believe it makes you different. This could be your sexual or gender identity, a mental health or addiction problem, your religion, or a particular belief or opinion you hold. Hiding that part of yourself protects you from being rejected by others. It's sometimes difficult to tell if shame is justified or not, because this emotion involves an element of knowing the opinions and values of others, and what they might think if they knew about this thing. For instance, many still attach stigma to mental illness, and if your best friend has previously told you about their coworker who "uses their depression as an excuse all the time," or they insist that there's "no such thing as mental illness," then you're likely to keep quiet about your emotional problems in order to avoid their judgment. On the other hand, if your boss has confided in you about their own anxious thoughts, or the fact that their child has been hospitalized for mental health problems, you'll be more certain that you can talk to them without fear of rejection.

More often than not, shame is not actually justified. It often comes up, though, because shame is the awful, soul-sucking feeling that we feel when we judge ourselves. So instead of thinking, *I shouldn't have said that to my partner* (causing guilt), you're thinking, *What kind of person am I that I said that to my partner?* or *I'm awful*. Judging yourself for something you've done or for something you feel is defective about you will cause you to feel shame.

We often confuse guilt and shame. One reason for this is that we often feel both at the same time, when we judge our behavior (leading to feelings of guilt) and we judge ourselves for having done that behavior (causing us to feel shame).

Examples of shame thoughts. When we feel ashamed, we're usually judging ourselves in some way: *I'm defective. There's something wrong with me. If others knew the real me they would* *leave. I'm an awful person. I'm a failure.* With shame there is also often an element of fearing that others will reject us.

Body sensations:
Pain in the pit of the stomach
Slumped posture, bowed head
Hot, flushed face
Sense of dread

Urges and behaviors. Shame can make you want to crawl under the nearest rock, hiding and isolating yourself from others. Taken to the extreme, it can cause thoughts of suicide. It can also be difficult to make eye contact with others when you're feeling shame.

Other words for feeling shame:
Mortified
Self-disgust
Self-loathing

There aren't really many other words for shame, although sometimes we use "embarrassed" or "humiliated" to describe the emotion, even though both are very different from shame. Think of "embarrassed" as the feeling we have when we trip up the stairs or walk out of the bathroom with TP stuck to our foot: when we're embarrassed, we can laugh at ourselves or the situation later. "Humiliation" is a little closer to shame, but it also involves anger—the sense of someone having caused us to feel shame when we didn't deserve it. In this sense, humiliation can be seen as more tolerable than shame because the anger drives us to talk to others about the situation and seek validation for our feelings, whereas shame keeps us disconnected and hiding.

Self-Inquiry: Shame

Think of a recent time when you felt shame, and describe the situation. What happened? What urges did you notice when you were in the situation you described? What did you actually do? Can you think of other words that fit better to describe what you experienced?

Envy

Envy and jealousy are two more emotions that are often confused with each other, but they are very distinct.

Envy's purpose. Envy is the emotion that usually comes up when an individual or group of people has something that you want.

What envy does. Healthy envy motivates us to work hard to get what we want. For example, if you envy a coworker who received recognition at work, it drives you to work harder so that you might also be recognized in some way. But envy can also play out in unhealthy urges, such as acting in ways to try to make the other person look bad to others, judging the person, trying to take away or ruin what the other person has, and so on.

Example of when envy is justified. You have feelings for your best friend's partner—that is, you envy your best friend for that relationship. If you were never part of the in-crowd at school, you may have been envious of the popular people (and this may still be happening!). Seeing someone who seems to have everything—lots of money, a great career, a beautiful house, a happy marriage—and wanting (understandably!) what that person has is justified.

Examples of envy thoughts. *It's not fair; why can't I have that? Why do they get all the luck and I get nothing but suffering in life?* When envy is accompanied by feelings of happiness for the other person, it can be quite healthy. As noted earlier, envy can motivate us to work hard to get the things we want: *I'm happy that my coworker got that promotion, but damn I wish that had been me!* When envy isn't accompanied by those feelings, but rather by feelings of anger, it can be detrimental and cause us to get stuck in feelings of self-pity and unhealthy behaviors.

Body sensations:

Tight or rigid muscles

Teeth clenching

Mouth tightening

Face flushing

Pain in the pit of the stomach

Urges and behaviors. Healthy urges and behaviors related to envy usually involve pushing yourself to do more and try harder to improve yourself and your situation. Unhealthy urges and behaviors related to envy include attacking or criticizing the person you envy; doing something to try to make that person fail, look bad to others, or lose what they have; or avoiding seeing or interacting with the person.

Other words for feeling envy:
Craving
Wanting
Resentful
Covetous
Desirous
Hunger
Longing

Self-Inquiry: Envy

Think of a recent time when you felt envy, and describe the situation. What happened? What urges did you notice when you were in the situation you described? What did you actually do? Can you think of other words that fit better to describe what you experienced?

Jealousy

Jealousy's purpose. Like all of the emotions we're looking at, jealousy is a basic emotion that has been identified in infants and can therefore be described as hardwired in the human brain. This emotion arises when an important relationship or sense of belonging is in danger of being lost or taken away.

What jealousy does. Jealousy typically causes people to try to control others in order to protect what's "theirs" (whether accurate or not!), and to not share the people or things they fear they'll lose.

Examples of when jealousy is justified. You find out that your partner has been talking to their ex. Or, you reached out to your three closest friends to see if they'd like to get together, but no one responded; then weeks later your best friend lets slip that they and those two other friends met last week without you—ouch.

Examples of jealousy thoughts. *They're going to leave me. No one cares about me. I'm going to lose everything.* Jealousy can also be thought of as anxiety about losing someone or something that's important to you.

Body sensations:

Racing heart

Breathlessness

Choking sensation

Lump in throat

Tense or tight muscles, such as clenching teeth

Urges and behaviors. Urges and behaviors associated with feeling jealous might involve being violent or threatening violence toward the person you feel threatened by; trying to control the person you're afraid of losing, including interrogating and spying on them and snooping through their belongings; accusing the person you're afraid of losing of being unfaithful or disloyal; behaving in a clinging, dependent way; or increasing demonstrations of love, like trying to spend more time together.

Other words for feeling jealousy:
Protective
Covetous
Clingy
Suspicious
Distrustful
Insecure
Possessive
Rivalrous

Self-Inquiry: Jealousy
　　Think of a recent time when you felt jealous, and describe the situation. What

happened? What urges did you notice when you were in the situation you described? What did you actually do? Can you think of other words that fit better to describe what you experienced?

Awareness of Emotions

Now that you have a better understanding of some of the painful emotions you might be experiencing, let's get you applying what you've learned by thinking about situations you encounter in your own life. The following questions will help you start to examine your emotions more closely, which will help you name the emotions accurately and understand them better.

Think about a situation that triggered an emotion for you. In your journal, answer the following questions. (Hint: You can do this for as many situations and emotions as you like!)

- Describe the situation (just the facts!).
- What thoughts did you have about this situation (including judgments, interpretations, assumptions)?
- What physical sensations did you notice?
- What urges did you experience?
- What did you actually do?
- What is the name of the emotion(s) you were experiencing?

As you answer these questions and get to know your experience of emotions better, it will be helpful for you to refer to the information about emotions we've just covered. For example, you may think you're feeling guilt but find, when you turn to the reference sheet on "guilt," that it doesn't quite match with your experience: you realize you're not judging your *behavior*, but *yourself*, and it's actually shame you're feeling. Over time, engaging in these exercises and reviewing the information about emotions will help improve your ability to identify what you're feeling. This next practice will further help you to label your emotions accurately.

Mindfulness of Emotions

This practice will help you recognize the different components of your emotions, so that over time you'll be able to accurately label them. To prepare for this practice (as well as the others in this book), you might want to read the script to yourself a couple of times so it comes more naturally for you. You might also choose to record yourself reading the scripts throughout the book so you can play them back until you get the hang of them; or you might have someone read them out loud to you.

Start by sitting in a comfortable position, taking a dignified posture: your back fairly straight against the chair, your feet flat on the floor. (If you have physical pain issues, just do your best to adopt a posture that you'll be able to stay in.) Take a couple of deep breaths. Our breathing can become shallow when we're having a strong emotion, so try to feel your belly expand as you inhale. When you're ready, let your attention slowly move through your body from your head to fingertips and toes, scanning your body for places you're holding tension. It's common to clench your jaw or to literally sit on the edge of your seat if you're feeling a difficult emotion, so just observe whatever is happening in your body.

Allow yourself to become aware of any emotion that's with you right now. (If you don't notice anything, continue to scan through your body until you do notice something, however small or neutral it might seem.) Where do you feel it most strongly? There might be one or several places in your body where you feel the emotion. Just be curious about the sensations, exploring them as best as you can with a sense of openness. It's natural to notice yourself wanting to avoid or resist the feelings and sensations, especially if they're uncomfortable, but see if you can be with them with acceptance and curiosity instead, just for a moment. Remember to breathe.

Now, see if you can put nonjudgmental words to your experience: describe what you notice in your body. For example, you might describe the quality of the feeling as "tight," "butterflies," "knot," or "hard;" describe the size of the feeling (small, medium, large); or notice a temperature to the emotion that you can label as "hot" or "cold" or somewhere in between. Go with whatever feels right; you're just listening to your body in this moment, observing the sensations that are present and the emotions they might reveal. You're not trying to make anything happen, nor are you trying to stop anything from happening.

You may be able to put a label on the emotion, like "grief," "shame," "bored," or "anxious." Label it if you can; if you can't put a name on it, just notice that. If you notice a thought or a story come up that's related to this emotion (for example, remembering something hurtful you did or said that has triggered feelings of shame for you), just notice that as best as you can without judging, and bring your attention back to whatever physical sensations are most prominent in your body right now.

If an emotion feels uncomfortable or distressing, see if you can just breathe into it, and continue to observe it, reminding yourself that it isn't permanent—emotions come and go.

If it gets to be too much, you can leave the practice and come back to it another time. Ultimately, you can do this practice (letting your thoughts and emotions go and staying connected with your body) for as short or long a time as you'd like.

In your journal, reflect on your experience doing this exercise by answering the following questions:
- As you did this exercise, what did you notice in your body?
- What did you notice about your thoughts?
- What did you notice about your emotions?
- Were you able to distinguish between the physical, mental, and emotional parts of your experience?
- Did you notice the emotions change in any way?
- Did you notice any thoughts that brought up or intensified an emotion or physical sensation?

Chapter 2

PAUSE AND OBSERVE

While naming our emotions accurately is important in helping us to tame them (Siegel 2014), pressing the *pause* button, so to speak, will also help us to choose how we want to respond in any situation, rather than just reacting from those emotions. In this chapter, you'll first learn some skills that will help you to detach from the emotion—you'll still feel it, of course, but in putting a little bit of distance between you and the emotion, it will no longer have the ability to control you.

In the second part of this chapter, you'll do some practices and learn skills to help you to not be hijacked by emotions. As you read through these skills and exercises, remember that the most important part of work like this is finding the skills that resonate for you, and putting them into practice on a regular basis in order to benefit from them in the long run. Now is a good time to start that list of skills in your journal. As you read through this book, pay attention to the skills that resonate for you in some way and that you're willing to try. On your list, you can include skills you already use to effectively help you tolerate distress as well as the new ones you're learning.

Skills to Quickly Regulate Emotions

Here are some strategies that activate certain systems in the human body to help you to hit that pause button. These strategies will allow you to quickly feel more emotionally balanced and able to make choices from a place of responsiveness rather than reactivity. When first learning these skills, it's usually most helpful to practice them before your emotions are really activated, so you know how to do them and what to expect. Once you have a handle on them, you can use them when emotions start to intensify. (Here's a tip, though: While these skills will still help when you're already in full-blown crisis mode, they'll be even more effective if you can catch yourself as emotions start to escalate, before you get really dysregulated.) These skills can help reduce many emotions, including anger, fear, anxiety, shame, and sadness.

The forward bend. Bend over as though you're trying to touch your toes, take some slow, deep breaths, and hang out there for thirty to sixty seconds if you can. This activates the parasympathetic nervous system (PNS), which acts as our body's brake, helping us to slow down and feel calmer. When you're ready, stand up again—slowly, so you don't fall over! It doesn't matter if you can actually touch your toes, and you can also do this sitting down if you need to by sticking your head between your knees. The key here is getting your head below your heart.

Focus on your exhale. It may sound cliché, but breathing is truly one of the best ways to calm intense emotions, and making your exhale longer than your inhale activates the PNS. As you inhale, count in your head; as you exhale, count at the same pace, making sure your exhale is at least a little bit longer than your inhale. For example, if you get to four when you inhale, make sure you exhale to at least five. By the way, pairing this exercise with the forward bend is a double whammy to challenging emotions, so while doing a forward bend, focus on making your exhale longer than your inhale.

Suck on lemons! Okay, so you don't actually have go that far, but sucking on a tart candy or eating something tart like salt-and-vinegar chips—or even *imagining* that you are (did your mouth just start to water?!)—stimulates the salivary glands, which are connected to our PNS. The long and short of it is that producing more saliva moves our body into the rest and digest PNS mode, helping us to feel calmer and come back down from that fight-or-flight state.

Activate your dive reflex. Putting your face in cold water activates a system in our body known as the *mammalian dive reflex* —another technique that can help you quickly break out of an intense emotion and get your emotions re-regulated (Linehan 2014). All mammals have this reflex; since we can't breathe under water, our body conserves oxygen by slowing down the heart. The good news for us humans is that this reflex can also help us to regulate our emotions—fast!

It's important to know that if you have a heart problem (including low blood pressure), are taking medications called "beta blockers," or have disordered eating (restricting or purging), you can't use this skill, so stop reading here! If you're not sure whether you can use this skill safely, check with your doctor before reading any further, because this skill can actually cause you to pass out. If you're 100 percent certain that these caveats do not apply to you, go to the nearest sink, fill it with cold water, and put your face in the water for thirty seconds (or as long as you can). If you're fearful of trying this technique, you can splash cold water on your face or hold an ice pack over your eyes instead, but to activate the dive reflex, it works best if you hold your breath and tip yourself forward to trick your body into thinking you're in water.

If you're not able to use this skill for whatever reason, you can still use temperature to help you manage emotions: whenever the body is required to adjust to cold temperatures, the SNS system turns off and the PNS is activated. This means that holding a cold compress or ice pack to your forehead, your wrists, or the back of your neck, for instance, will still help.

Intense exercise. Most people know that there's an association between aerobic exercise and emotional well-being, but the nature of this link is still not well understood (Bernstein and McNally 2017). We do know that intense exercise boosts certain chemicals in our brain, reducing emotional pain and improving our mood and our ability to manage emotions. Here's what this connection boils down to: if you're stressed out and emotions are beginning to overwhelm you, do some jumping jacks or lunges in your bedroom, go for a run around the block, or run up and down your stairs. As with the other skills in this section, doing so will help interrupt a cycle of feelings, thoughts, and behaviors that might otherwise take over, opening space for you to respond to what you're feeling in a healthier, more adaptive way.

Acupressure points. This is another skill that doesn't take a lot of thought or practice; you just have to remember to do it when emotions get intense. Many people are already familiar with using acupressure points to treat physical pain, but acupressure points can also help us feel a little calmer when emotions start to spike. The LI4 acupressure point, between your thumb and your index finger, activates endorphins in the body that help reduce stress. Using the index finger and thumb of your right hand, gently pinch the cushy part between the index finger and thumb of your left hand; use a deep, firm pressure to massage and stimulate the area for four to five seconds (you can also massage your right hand with your left).

Another acupressure point is located just under our collarbone. Massaging the little indent directly underneath the collarbone, between the breastbone and shoulder, can also help us to feel a little calmer. You can massage either side alone, or do both sides at once, adding in a bit of a self-hug, which can't do anything but help! And, incorporating paced breathing, which you already learned, with this self-massage will further activate a calming response in your body.

Skills to Prevent Dysregulation

Now you have some skills to use that will help you hit that pause button and reduce the likelihood of you reacting in problematic ways when emotions start to get intense. Next, let's move to some exercises that are more preventative, and will keep you from getting to that dysregulated state in the first place.

The First Doorway to Spirit: Your Breath

For thousands of years, the breath has been used as a focus for meditation. This is no accident, because breath is the *source*, the center, of your physical life. The in and out of each breath, as it holds your attention, can do three important things that strengthen your spiritual awareness:

1. Breath-focused meditation quiets emotions. A large body of scientific research demonstrates the power of meditation to soften intense feelings, so you become less emotionally driven and overwhelmed. Even meditating two to five minutes a day can make a difference, because you learn to *watch* your feelings instead of being carried away by them.
2. Breath-focused meditation allows you to observe and distance yourself from thoughts. Runaway thoughts, in the form of rumination and worry, play a major role in human distress, and they can occupy your mind to the point that spiritual awareness gets lost. Meditation teaches you to merely watch thoughts rather than get lost in them; to quiet your mind so you can listen to spirit.
3. Breath-focused meditation creates awareness of the moment of choice and strengthens your ability to choose wisely. The moment of choice occurs when painful or distressing thoughts and emotions gang up and start driving you to do something—anything—to get rid of the pain. Pain-driven actions are often damaging; over time they have a

corrosive effect. Meditation can strengthen your ability to see the alternative, wise actions you could take instead.

The way you breathe is very important. The way we're going to suggest that you breathe might feel unnatural at first. But do your best to be patient, and don't judge yourself or give up.

Most of us were never taught "how" to breathe. We just did it from birth. However, many of us have picked up some unhelpful habits that might be interfering with our ability to relax and focus. So, right now, as you're reading this, put one hand on your chest and one hand on your belly. Notice which hand moves more. Many people will notice the hand on the chest moves more, and might even notice that the body tends to rock or sway as they breathe in and out. This is not the most efficient or effective way to breathe; instead, ideally, you should be breathing with the support of your *diaphragm*, the muscle at the bottom of your rib cage. When the diaphragm moves down toward your belly button, it causes your lungs to fill with air. However, in order for it to move easily and properly, you have to release your abdominal muscles and allow them to expand, rather than hold them tight and rigid. (Look at the way an infant breathes for a good example—all the movement is in the belly, without any upper chest rocking.) This is called *diaphragmatic breathing*, breathing that activates the diaphragm muscle at the bottom of your lung cavity. As you continue to hold one hand on your chest and one hand on your belly, do your best to mentally shift the movement you feel to your abdominal area. As you slowly breathe in, allow your belly to gently inflate like a balloon, and as you slowly exhale, allow your belly to gently and effortlessly deflate. The key here is to take "slow" breaths, *not* "deep" breaths. You do *not* have to fill up your entire lung capacity when you breathe. Rather, allow yourself to find a slow steady rhythm that allows a natural amount of air in and out of your body. (If you breathe too deeply or too rapidly you might start to feel light-headed, dizzy, or tingly in your lips or fingertips; this means you're hyperventilating. If so, stop the practice, relax, recover, and try again later using a slower, steadier rhythm. Try imagining an ocean wave slowly moving in to the shore and then slowly retreating, and you'll probably find a slow, steady rhythm.) It might take some time to make this transition from upper chest breathing to diaphragmatic breathing, but don't give up—it's worth it.

Cue-Controlled Relaxation

Cue-controlled relaxation is a quick and easy technique that will help you reduce your stress level and muscle tension. A *cue* is a trigger or command that helps you relax. In this case, your cue will be a word, like "relax" or "peace." The goal of this technique is to train your body to release muscle tension when you think about your cue word. Initially, you'll need the help of the guided instructions to help you release muscle tension in different sections of your body. But once you've been practicing this technique for some time, you'll be able to relax your whole body at once, simply by taking a few slow breaths and thinking about your cue word. With practice, this can become a very quick and easy technique to help you relax. Before you begin, choose a cue word that will help you relax. Write your word in your journal.

To begin this exercise, find a comfortable chair to sit in. Once you've been practicing this exercise for some time, you'll be able to do it wherever you are, even if you're standing. You'll also be able to do it more quickly. But to begin, choose a comfortable place to sit in a place where you won't be disturbed. Make sure you'll be free from distractions. Turn off your phone, television, computer, and radio. Tell the people in your home, if there are any, that you can't be disturbed for the next twenty minutes. Allow yourself the time and the freedom to relax. You deserve it.

To begin, sit in a comfortable chair with your feet flat on the floor and your hands resting comfortably, either on the arms of the chair or in your lap. Close your eyes. Take a slow, long breath in through your nose. Feel your belly expand like a balloon as you breathe in. Hold it for five seconds: 1, 2, 3, 4, 5. Then, release it slowly through your mouth. Feel your belly collapse like a balloon losing its air. Again, take a slow, long breath in through your nose and feel your stomach expand. Hold it for five seconds: 1, 2, 3, 4, 5. Then, exhale slowly through your mouth. One more time: take a slow, long breath in through your nose and feel your stomach expand. Hold it for five seconds: 1, 2, 3, 4, 5. Then, exhale slowly through your mouth. Now, begin to take slow, long breaths without holding them, and continue to breathe smoothly for the rest of this exercise.

Now, with your eyes still closed, imagine that a beam of light (it can be any color that feels soothing to you) shines down from the sky like a bright laser and lands on the very top of your head. Notice how warm and soothing the light feels. This could be a light from God, the universe, or whatever power makes you feel comfortable. As you continue to breathe smoothly, taking slow, long breaths, notice how the light makes you feel more and more relaxed as it continues to shine on the top of your head. Now, slowly, the warm light begins to spread over the top of your head like soothing water. And as it does, the light begins to loosen any muscle tension that you're feeling on the top of your head. Slowly, the light begins to slide down your body, and as it moves across your forehead, all the muscle tension there is released. Then the light continues down past your ears, the back of your head, your eyes, nose, mouth, and chin, and it continues to release any tension you're holding there. Notice how pleasantly warm your forehead feels. Now, slowly, imagine that the light begins to move down your neck and over your shoulders, releasing any muscle tension. Then the light slowly proceeds down both of your arms and the front and back of your torso. Feel the muscles in your upper and lower back release. Notice the soothing sensation of the light as it moves across your chest and stomach. Feel the muscles in your arms release as the light moves down to your forearms and then across both sides of your hands to your fingertips. Now, notice the light moving down through your pelvis and buttocks and feel the tension being released. Again, feel the light move like soothing water across your upper and lower legs until it spreads across both the upper and lower surfaces of your feet. Feel all of the tension leaving the muscles of your body as the light makes your body feel warm and relaxed.

Continue to notice how peaceful and calm you feel as you continue to take slow, long, smooth breaths. Observe how your stomach continues to expand as you inhale, and feel it deflate as you exhale. Now, as you continue breathing, think to yourself, *Breathe in,* as you inhale, and then think your cue word as you exhale. (If your cue word is something other than "relax," use that word in the following instructions.) Slowly inhale and think: *Breathe in.* Slowly exhale and think: *Relax.* As you do this, notice your entire body feeling relaxed at the same time. Feel all the muscle tension in your body being released as you focus on your cue word. Again, inhale and think: *Breathe in.* Exhale and think: *Relax.* Notice your entire body releasing any muscle tension. Again, inhale ... *Breathe in.* Exhale ... *Relax.* Feel all the tension in your body releasing.

Continue breathing and thinking these words at your own pace for several minutes. With each breath, notice how relaxed your entire body feels. When your mind begins to wander, return your focus to the words "breathe in" and "relax."

Practice the cue-controlled relaxation technique twice a day, and record how long it takes you to feel relaxed. With daily practice, this technique should help you relax more quickly each time. Again, remember that the ultimate goal of this technique is to train your entire body to relax simply when you think of your cue word, such as "relax." This will only come with regular practice. Initially, you might also have to think of the light imagery and engage in slow, deep breathing to help yourself relax. But with practice, this technique can help you relax even in distressing situations.

Acceptance Meditation

This Acceptance Meditation is inspired by Neff and Germer's (date unknown) "Soften, soothe, allow" meditation. Practicing this meditation as soon as you notice distressing physical sensations or emotions will help you to manage the discomfort more effectively and press pause to prevent yourself from reacting. But it will also be important to take time to practice this meditation (about fifteen minutes), at least once a day, so that you'll be more able to use it in times of distress.

Begin by getting into a comfortable sitting position. Close your eyes and focus on your breath. Bring your attention to your diaphragm, the center of your breath and life force. Notice each in-breath and mark it by thinking to yourself, *In*. Notice each out-breath and mark it by thinking to yourself, *Out*. Continue watching your breath, thinking *In* and *Out*. (Pause here)

As you focus on your breath, thoughts will likely begin to arise—memories, worries, plans for the future, judgments. Just notice the thoughts and, as soon as you can, return to your breath. (Pause here) Just watch the breath, letting it rise and fall gently and effortlessly. A slow, natural rhythm. (Pause two minutes)

At this moment, let your attention expand beyond your breath. Let yourself notice where the tension or difficult emotion manifests in your body. You might notice tension, pain, an itch, or just a strange sensation in your body. Do your best to just notice it without judgment, and place your attention there for a moment. (Pause here)

Next, soften toward that tension or difficult emotion in your body. Allow the muscles to release around it. Just notice the physical sensation or emotion without trying to control it, without trying to push it away. Your body can be soft around the edges of the feeling, making room for it. Letting go ... letting go ... letting go of tension around the edges of the feeling. (Pause here)

As you're observing, if you experience too much discomfort from an emotion, do your best to note your experience and return to the rising and falling of your breath; use your breath as your anchor. Do your best not to judge your emotion and not to get distracted by it. (Pause here)

Similarly, if a difficult thought arises, do your best to just notice it and let it go. Again, return to the rising and falling of your breath as your anchor. Do your best not to judge yourself or the thought. (Pause here)

Now, hold the physical sensation or emotion kindly. Move your hand to cover and hold the spot. Breathe into that feeling. Breathe in a kind regard for that tension or difficult emotion. Think of this place as yours to take care of, to hold as if it were precious and needing your love. (Pause here)

Again, if a difficult thought arises, or your mind wanders, notice and accept it. Then, let it go. (Pause here)

Let this physical sensation or emotion be. Let it be there without resistance. Let it go or stay. Let it change or not change. Let it be where it is or move. Let it be what it is, making room for it, holding it, accepting its presence in your body and your life. (Pause here)

Soften ... hold ... let be. Soften ... hold ... let be. Soften ... hold ... let be. Repeat these words to yourself, holding any pain you may have kindly. Allowing it to stay or leave or change. (Pause here) As you continue, allow difficult thoughts to arise—just noticing them and letting them go. (Pause here)

As you continue, you may find that the emotion moves in your body, or even changes into another emotion. Try staying with your experience, continuing to use the mantra of soften-hold-let be. (Pause here)

Finally, return your attention to your breath, simply noticing the rising and falling of your breath: breathe in and breathe out. Then, when you are ready, slowly open your eyes. (Close the meditation)

Keep practicing the Acceptance Meditation daily. Its transformative effect takes time, but you should notice over a period of six to twelve weeks that emotions and feelings disturb you less. They're just part of the ever-changing present. You hold them and merely wait. The pain, always and eventually, becomes something else—some new experience—that you can welcome and hold until the next new thing shows up.

Where Am I Now? Overcoming Thoughts of the Future and the Past

The next time you're in a distressing or difficult situation, ask yourself the following questions:
- *Where am I right now?*

- *Am I time traveling in the future, worrying about or imagining something that might happen?*
- *Am I time traveling in the past, reliving mistakes, rehashing bad experiences, or thinking about how my life could have been under different circumstances?*
- *Or am I in the present, really paying attention to what I'm doing, thinking and feeling?*

If you're not in the present moment, refocus your attention on what's happening to you now by using the following steps:

- Notice what you're thinking about and recognize if you're time traveling. Bring your focus back to the present moment.
- Notice how you're breathing. Take slow, long breaths to help you refocus on the present.
- Notice how your body feels and observe any tension or pain you might be feeling. Recognize how your thoughts might be contributing to how you're feeling. Use cue-controlled relaxation to release any tension.
- Notice any painful emotions you might be feeling as a result of time traveling, and use one of the distress tolerance skills (such as an activity to distract or self-soothe; more about these skills in later chapters!) to help you relieve any immediate pain.

Mindfulness of the Present Moment in Daily Life

You may have heard the word *mindfulness* thrown about here and there—it's used often nowadays; but what does it really mean? The definition of mindfulness is doing one thing at a time, in the present moment, with your full attention, and with acceptance. The more you stay in the present moment, the less you'll worry and ruminate. The less you judge, the less emotional suffering you create for yourself.

To begin integrating mindfulness into your daily life, choose to apply it to something you do briefly every day. It could be taking a shower, doing the dishes, drinking coffee, walking to the bus stop, eating breakfast, or helping your children get dressed. The activity should be physical, not mental, so you can focus on each detail of the experience. For example, if you've chosen doing the dishes as an opportunity for daily mindfulness, you'd focus on the feeling of hot water on your hands. Notice the sensations of holding the sponge and feeling the soap. Pay attention to the texture of the dish in your hands and the sensation of the water as you rinse it.

It doesn't matter what activity you choose. The point is to listen to what all your senses tell you. What you see, hear, feel, smell, and taste are the cornerstones of mindfulness. When thoughts arise, notice and label them, then return your attention to the sensory details of the activity you've chosen.

Practice doing your activity mindfully for a week. Sometimes it helps to put up signs or reminders to cue you to do the exercise. For example, a plan to do the dishes mindfully is more likely to happen if you put a sign over the sink. A plan to eat breakfast mindfully would be supported by a sign on the refrigerator, a carton of milk, or something else you typically consume at breakfast. If you plan to take a mindful walk to the bus stop, tie a piece of string on your briefcase or backpack as a reminder.

After the first week, add a second mindful activity and use a similar reminder system to help you follow through. Continue to add new mindful activities to your routine every week until you have a number of them peppered throughout your day.

While all mindfulness exercises will help you reduce negative thinking, you will still have moments when painful thoughts show up. Whenever that happens, slow down, make sure you're doing just one thing, and then pay attention to the physical activity you're engaged in. Notice only that activity and nothing else. Let yourself get immersed in what you're doing by paying attention to what your senses tell you.

Doing one thing at a time in the present moment, with your full attention, and with acceptance, helps slow you down, quiet your thoughts, and prevent extra emotional pain from arising; it will help you shift from thoughts about the future and the past to what's happening right now.

Choosing Your Mind's Focus

With more flexible thinking skills, you can choose what you think about. When negative thoughts show up, your first choice is now or later. If the thought feels compelling and you choose to think about it now, so be it. Any time you get tired of the thought, you can practice letting it go, disconnecting from it, and making room for another focus (for instance, mindfully noticing the thought; or reminding yourself, *It's just a thought, it's not a fact*) . You can also delay worry and rumination, setting a later time for those thoughts (writing them down to make sure you don't forget).

The next choice is what your alternative focus will be. Usually the best alternative focus is the present moment. Paying attention to your experience right now—everything your senses tell you about this moment—leaves little room for worry and rumination. Here are some other choices for an alternative mental focus:

- Planning
- Problem solving
- Pleasant reminiscing
- Daydreaming about positive future events
- Creative activities
- Pleasure activities
- Exercise
- Reading and learning
- Communicating and connecting with others

Remember, you control where your attention goes—so choose a focus that promotes your mental well-being!

Chapter 3

SOOTHE AND CALM USING YOUR SENSES AND BODY

Self-soothing, finding ways to calm ourselves, is another important skill that contributes to our ability to manage emotions effectively. While finding ways of soothing and calming ourselves can be helpful in the middle of a difficult situation and help us reduce the intensity of painful emotions, activities that soothe and calm us are generally also good *self-care* skills. And of course, the more care we take of ourselves, the more we'll be able to manage intense emotions as they arise.

In this chapter, you'll learn about how to self-soothe using each of the five senses, as well as a variety of practices to help you feel calmer; and you'll see many examples of how you might do this. Of course you won't relate to all of the examples, so what's most important is that you be thinking about what activities are soothing for you, and add them to your list in your journal.

Self-Soothing Using Your Sense of Vision

Vision is very important to humans. In fact, a large portion of our brain is devoted solely to our sense of sight. The things we look at can have very powerful effects on us, for better or for worse, making it important to find sights that are soothing to help you manage emotions. As already mentioned, for each person, it comes down to individual taste and preference. Here are some ideas. Add any of these activities you'd be willing to do, and any others that you can think of, to your list:

- Go through magazines and books to cut out pictures that you like. Make a collage of them to hang on your wall, or use a soothing picture for the wallpaper on your phone.
- Go to a place that's soothing for you to look at, like a park or a museum, or find a picture of a place that's soothing for you to look at, like the ocean.
- Go to the bookstore and find a collection of photographs or paintings that you find relaxing, such as nature photographs.
- Draw or paint your own picture that's pleasing to you.

- Carry a picture or photograph of someone you love, someone you find attractive, or someone you admire.

Self-Soothing Using Your Sense of Smell

Smell is a very powerful sense that can often trigger memories and make you feel a certain way. Therefore, it's very important that you identify smells that are pleasurable for you. Here are some ideas; add the ones you're willing to do, and any others that you can think of, to your list:

- Burn scented candles or incense in your room or house. Find a scent that's pleasing to you.
- Wear scented oils, lotion, perfume, or cologne that makes you feel happy, confident, or sexy.
- Cut out perfumed cards from magazines and carry them with you.
- Go someplace where the scent is pleasing to you, like a bakery or restaurant.
- Bake your own food that has a pleasing smell, like chocolate chip cookies.
- Go to a park or forest and inhale the smells of nature.
- Buy fresh-cut flowers or seek out flowers in your neighborhood.

- Hug someone you know whose smell makes you feel calm.

Self-Soothing Using Your Sense of Hearing

Certain sounds can soothe us. Listening to gentle music, for example, may be relaxing. However, everyone has different responses to music, so it's important that find what works best for you. Use the following examples to identify the sounds that will help you with different emotions. Add the ones you're willing to do, and any others you can think of, to your list:
- Listen to music. Identify the emotion you're experiencing, and consider what music might work best to help you manage that emotion. If you're feeling anxious, you might find jazz music calms you; if you're feeling sad, you might want something more energetic or upbeat. Listen to a wide variety of genres to determine which ones might be most helpful for you with different emotions. Then, download the music on your phone so you can listen to it anywhere you want.
- Listen to audiobooks. Many public libraries will let you borrow books on CDs or temporarily download audiobooks. Borrow a few to see if they help you relax. You don't

even have to pay attention to the storyline. Sometimes just listening to the sound of someone talking can be very relaxing. Again, keep some of these recordings on your phone so you can access them when you need them.
- Turn on the television and just listen. Find a show that's boring or sedate, not something that might be agitating like the news. Sit in a comfortable chair or lie down, and then close your eyes and just listen. Make sure you turn the volume down to a level that's not too loud. Many years ago, there was a show on public television featuring a painter named Bob Ross. His voice was so soothing and relaxing that many people reported falling asleep while watching him. Find a show like this that will help you relax.
- Listen to a soothing podcast or video online, or find a soothing talk show on the radio. Remember—a *soothing* podcast or talk show, not something that's going to make you stressed or angry. Again, stay away from political talk shows and the news. Find something neutral or perhaps interesting in discussion, like the *TED Talks* series online or *This American Life* on public radio. Again, sometimes just listening to someone else talk can be relaxing. Bookmark the links or download your favorite podcasts on your

phone so you can listen to them when you're feeling a difficult emotion.
- Open your window and listen to the peaceful sounds outside. Or, if you live in a place without calming sounds outside, go visit a place with soothing sounds, such as a park.
- Listen to a recording of nature sounds, such as birds and other wildlife. You can often download these online and then take them wherever you go.
- Listen to white noise. *White noise* is a sound that blocks out other distracting sounds. You can buy a machine that makes white noise with circulating air, turn on a fan to block out distracting sounds, stream a white noise video on your computer, or download a white-noise app on your smartphone. Some white-noise machines and apps even have other recorded sounds on them, such as the sounds of birds, water falls, and rainforests, which you might find soothing.
- Listen to the sound of a water fountain. Many people find the sound of the trickling water from these small electronic fountains to be very soothing.
- Listen to a meditation or relaxation exercise. Exercises such as these will help you imagine yourself relaxing in many different ways. Other recorded exercises can even teach you

self-hypnosis techniques to help you relax. Recordings like these can be found online; you can take the programs with you on your phone to listen to whenever you're feeling overwhelmed. (Just don't listen to them while you're driving or operating equipment, when it might be dangerous if you fell asleep.) Call someone you care about and speak to them for a few minutes; just hearing the voice of loved ones can be soothing. If this is something you know is soothing for you, you might even ask your loved one to record a message that you can listen to when they're not available.

Self-Soothing Using Your Sense of Taste

Taste is another very powerful sense. Our sensations of flavor can trigger memories and emotions, so again, it's important that you find the tastes that are pleasing to you. If eating is a problem for you, such as eating too much, bingeing, purging, or restricting what you eat, talk to a professional counselor about getting help for yourself. If the process of eating can be stressful for you, use your other senses to calm yourself. But if taste soothes you, use some of these suggestions. Add the ones you're willing

to do, and any others you can think of, to your list:
- Enjoy your favorite meal, whatever it is. Eat it slowly so you can enjoy the way it tastes.
- Carry lollipops, gum, or other candy with you to eat when you're feeling a difficult emotion.
- Eat a soothing food, like ice cream, chocolate, pudding, or something else that gives you pleasure.
- Drink something soothing, such as tea, coffee, or hot chocolate. Practice drinking it slowly so you can enjoy the way it tastes.
- Suck on an ice cube or an ice pop, especially if you're feeling warm, and enjoy the taste as it melts in your mouth.
- Buy a piece of juicy, fresh fruit and then eat it slowly.

Self-Soothing Using Your Sense of Touch

We often forget about our sense of touch, and yet we're always touching something, such as the clothes we're wearing or the chair we're sitting in. Our skin is our largest organ, and it's completely covered with nerves that carry feelings to our brain. Certain tactile sensations can be pleasing, like petting our dog or cat, while other sensations shock or cause pain in order to communicate danger, like touching a hot stove.

Again, each of us prefers different sensations, so you'll have to figure out which are the ones that are most pleasing for you. Here are some suggestions. Add the ones you're willing to do, and any others you can think of, to your list:

- Carry something in your pocket to touch when you need to, like a piece of soft cloth or a smooth stone.
- Take a warm or cold shower and enjoy the feeling of the water falling on your skin.
- Take a warm bubble bath or a bath with scented oils and enjoy the soothing sensations on your skin.
- Get a massage. Many people who have survived physical and sexual abuse do not want to be touched by anyone. This is understandable. But not all types of massage require you to take off your clothes, which may feel safer. Some techniques, such as traditional Japanese shiatsu massage, simply require you to wear loose-fitting clothes. A shoulder and neck massage, received while seated in a massage chair, can also be done without removing any clothes.
- Massage yourself, or rub some lotion into your skin. Sometimes just rubbing your own sore muscles is very pleasing.
- Play with your pet. Owning a pet can have many health benefits. Pet owners often have

lower blood pressure, lower cholesterol levels, and reduced risk for heart disease (Anderson, Reid, and Jennings 1992), and they also experience other general health improvements (Serpell 1991). In addition, playing with your pet and stroking the animal's fur or skin can provide you with a soothing tactile experience. If you don't have a pet, consider getting one. Or if you can't afford one or if you can't have one where you live, visit a friend who has a pet or volunteer at your local animal shelter, where you can play with the rescued animals.

- Wear your most comfortable clothes, like your favorite worn-in T-shirt, baggy sweat suit, or old jeans.

Half-Smile

There is a saying that "sometimes your joy is the source of your smile, but sometimes your smile is the source of your joy." Research has shown that changing our facial expression can influence our mood (Ekman and Davidson 1993). The idea behind the half-smile (Linehan 2014) is that by slightly turning the corners of our mouth up—try for less than the *Mona Lisa*—we can improve our sense of well-being. The half-smile is a very slight smile—so slight that if you're looking at yourself in a mirror you might not be able to see it, but you *feel* it. Let me clarify that this isn't a fake smile, which creates tension in the muscles in our face that *reduces* our sense of well-being. If you're struggling to find the balance with this expression, bite down on a pen; doing so will turn the corners of your mouth up slightly. Give the half-smile a try the next time you notice emotional pain arising. Try it with different emotions at different times.

Taking an Open Posture

Our mind and body are irrevocably connected, so adopting a willing posture increases our receptiveness to an experience by influencing our mind to be more accepting and willing.

Sitting with your back fairly straight and your feet flat on the floor (if that's comfortable), tune in to your breath. Notice how it feels to breathe, drawing the air in through your nose. If you can, deepen your breathing. Feel the air expand your lungs as you inhale, and notice your lungs deflate as you exhale through your mouth or your nose, whichever is more comfortable.

Now, turn your attention to the rest of your body, noticing your posture and slowly opening it up:

Roll your shoulders back.

Open up your heart by pointing your chest toward the ceiling.

Open your hands wide, spreading your fingers as far apart as you can.

If you'd like, sweep your arms over your head and reach for the sky, keeping your fingers wide.

For additional willingness, add the half-smile skill you just learned!

Notice when your attention wanders, and gently, without judging, return your attention to the present—the feel of your breath and your body opening up. Continue to breathe and maintain this willing, open posture for as long or as short a time as you'd like. Don't forget to add this and the half-smile to your list of distress tolerance skills if they're ones you're willing to try!

You can practice this mindfulness exercise when you find yourself feeling willful or struggling to accept something, or just for the sake of practicing. The more you practice, the more willing and accepting you'll feel on a regular basis, and the more you'll be able to get to that willing attitude when you want or need to. Don't forget, if these skills resonate with you, add them to your list!

Mindful Breathing Meditation

Another exercise that will help you stay focused in the present moment is breathing. It sounds simple, but we often don't breathe as well as we should. Think about it: Who taught you how to breathe? If you're like the rest of us, probably no one. And yet, you do it about fifteen times a minute or almost twenty-two thousand times a day! Everyone knows that we breathe air to take in oxygen. But how much of the air you breathe is actually oxygen—100 percent, 75 percent? The correct answer is that the air you breathe is only about 21 percent oxygen, and when your body doesn't get enough oxygen it can knock your biological system off balance. For this reason alone, taking full, slow breaths is important. But another benefit of breathing correctly is that this simple technique can help you relax and focus. Many spiritual traditions combine slow breathing techniques with guided meditations to help people focus and relax.

Here's another diaphragmatic breathing exercise that many people find helpful. Engaging the diaphragm helps you take fuller, deeper breaths, which helps you relax.

Set a timer for three to five minutes and practice breathing until the alarm goes off. Then, as you get more accustomed to using this technique to help you relax, you can set the alarm for longer periods of time, like ten or fifteen minutes. But don't expect to be able to sit still that long when you first start. In the beginning, three to five minutes is a long time to sit still and breathe. When using this new form of breathing, many people often feel as if they become "one" with their breathing, meaning that they feel a deep connection to the experience. If that happens for you, great. If not, that's okay too. Just keep practicing. Also, some people feel light-headed when they first begin practicing this technique. This may be caused by breathing too fast, too deeply, or too slowly. Don't be alarmed. If you begin to feel light-headed, stop if you need to, or return your breathing to a normal rate and begin counting your breaths.

To begin, find a comfortable place to sit where you won't be disturbed. Turn off your phone and anything else that might be distracting. Take a few slow, long breaths and relax. Place one hand on your stomach and imagine your belly filling up with air as you breathe instead of your lungs. Now, slowly breathe in through your nose and slowly exhale through your mouth as if you're blowing out birthday candles. Feel your stomach rise and fall as you breathe. Imagine your belly filling up with air like a balloon as you breathe in, and then feel it effortlessly deflate as you breathe out. Feel the breath moving in across your nostrils, and then feel your breath blowing out across your lips. As you breathe, notice the sensations in your body. Feel your lungs fill up with air. Notice the weight of your body resting on whatever you're sitting on. With each breath, notice how your body feels more and more relaxed.

Now, as you continue to breathe, begin counting your breaths each time you exhale. You can count either silently to yourself or aloud. Count each exhalation until you reach 4 and then begin counting at 1 again. To begin, breathe in slowly through your nose and then exhale slowly through your mouth. Count 1. Again, breathe in slowly through your nose and slowly out through your mouth. Count 2. Repeat, breathing in slowly through your nose, and then slowly exhale. Count 3. Last time—breathe in through your nose and out through your mouth. Count 4. Now, begin counting at 1 again.

When your mind begins to wander and you catch yourself thinking of something else, return your focus to counting your breaths. Try not to judge yourself for getting distracted. Just keep taking slow breaths into your belly, in and out. Feel your belly rising with each inhalation and falling with each exhalation. Keep counting each breath, and with each exhale, feel your body relaxing, deeper and deeper.

Keep breathing until your alarm goes off, and then slowly return your focus to the room.

Relaxation Without Tension (Body Awareness)

The relaxing effect of this exercise relies on the fact that you can't feel tense and nervous when all your muscles are in a state of relaxation.

Find a quiet spot where you can lie down and not be disturbed. Lie on your back with your legs uncrossed and your hands at your sides. Close your eyes. Take a long, slow breath, and bring your attention to your feet. Become aware of any tension you're feeling in your feet. Say to yourself, *Calm, Relax, Serene, Easy,* or another cue word of your choice. As you say the cue word, imagine any tension draining out of your feet.

Next, move your attention up to your calves and shins. Notice any tension in your lower legs, and say your cue word to yourself. As you say the word to yourself, imagine any tension draining out of your calves and shins.

Now, do the same thing with your upper legs—the large muscles in your thighs. Continue moving your relaxing attention up your body: to your buttocks, then your stomach, then your chest, then your back, and then your shoulders. For each area of the body, become aware of any tension, then say your cue word and let the tension fade away.

Turn your attention now to your hands, then your forearms, your upper arms, your neck, and finally your head, in each case noticing any tension and using your cue word to dissolve the tension. When you've scanned your entire body in this way, you should have significantly reduced your overall muscular tension, profoundly relaxing your body.

Practicing this exercise once or twice a day for a week will teach you a lot about where you carry tension in your body. It will also make you much more adept at relaxation.

Chapter 4

BE KIND TO YOURSELF

While part of tolerating distress of course is managing the pain we experience in life, another part of it is learning to increase the pleasure. When things are stressful and chaotic, it can be easy to overlook moments of calm, peace, contentment, and even enjoyment—even more so when you're experiencing a lot of emotional pain or distress. Take a moment right now to consider the moments in your life when you might experience some kind of small pleasurable moment: your dog greets you at the door with unconditional love; you take a few minutes to sit outside on a sunny day; sharing a hug with your partner or child, or a smile with a stranger. How often do you think you miss noticing these moments? With practice, you'll be more able to notice the pleasure in life, even when it's only there for a short time or when the pleasurable emotion isn't an intense one like happiness or joy.

In this chapter, we'll look at some skills to help us do exactly that: generate pleasure, and really experience the pleasure when it's present, rather than missing out on it. The first set of skills will focus on changing our body chemistry to help us create those pleasurable emotions;

and then we'll turn our focus to changing thoughts and behaviors. Remember as you read through these skills to continue to add to your list of distress tolerance skills.

Activities That Generate Pleasurable Emotions

The following list of activities are proven to change our body chemistry to help us feel good. Of course, not every skill will fit every person, so you're going to need to try them out to figure out which ones work best for you.

Get out in nature. Just twenty minutes of exposure to a natural forest setting has been shown to significantly reduce a digestive enzyme called salivary alpha amylase, which is a marker of stress. Compared to a group sitting in a city park with no trees, study participants who sat in the woods experienced an eightfold decrease in salivary alpha amylase and reported significantly less stress (Beil and Hanes 2013).

Humming, chanting, and singing. Humming, chanting a mantra, and energetic singing increase heart rate variability (HRV), which is an indicator of the body's stress level. A low HRV means you're more stressed, whereas a high HRV means you're less stressed. In addition, singing at the top of your lungs works the muscles in the back of the throat to activate the vagus nerve, one of the main components of the parasympathetic nervous system (PNS). And singing with others offers a double whammy, as it generates oxytocin, known as the "love hormone" because it makes people feel more connected to one another! Oxytocin also calms the amygdala, the part of our brain responsible for emotional hijack, and temporarily prevents the release of stress hormones.

Reach out for physical connection. Hugging and holding hands releases oxytocin and reduces stress and feelings of loneliness. Even a pat on the back or a friendly handshake will help!

Laughter. Laughter also stimulates the vagus nerve, activating the PNS, and research has shown that when we laugh with a group of people our HRV increases, indicating lower stress levels (Dolgoff-Kaspar et al. 2012). So read the funny pages, turn on the comedy channel, or look into laughing yoga or laughing meditation—yep, both are a thing!

Listen to music. Research has found that areas of the brain release dopamine—known as the "feel-good neurotransmitter"—when we listen to our favorite music. So yes, there's a biological reason why music makes us feel good!

Having Compassion Helps

Compassion is defined as having an awareness and understanding of the emotional distress of others, along with a desire to alleviate it. As a result, compassion motivates us to help and support others, and it turns out this is good for our mental health! Research has shown that practices that increase compassion improve our relationships with others, which of course makes sense when we're bringing more compassion to those individuals; but even if we don't know the people for whom we're feeling compassion, this practice stimulates positive attitudes and feelings of kindness (Frostadottir and Dorjee 2019). This happens because, when we start practicing compassion, the brain activates circuits related to positive feelings. This may indicate that the more compassionate we are, the more often these types of feelings awaken in us. As a result, our ability to experience self-compassion also increases, reducing symptoms of depression, anxiety, self-criticism, and the feeling of inferiority.

So how do we increase our ability to be compassionate? Here is an exercise to help get you started.

Create a Compassion Awareness Journal

For the next week, pay attention to moments when you felt compassion—for yourself or someone else.

In your journal, answer the following questions:
- Describe the situation that triggered your compassion.

- What allowed this feeling to bloom? Was there a way you turned compassion into action? What exactly happened? (For example, you listened to a friend having a hard time or did a small kindness for a stranger.) Note: When there isn't a compassionate action, that's okay. Make no judgment about it. But be aware that a compassionate action is often possible and grows from the intention that you and others be free of suffering.
- Next, take a look at how compassion felt to you in this situation.

If there was self-compassion:
- Did you pause to appreciate and validate your own struggle?
- Did you ask for support? Did you tell someone what you're going through?

Loving-Kindness

Practicing loving-kindness, which is a form of mindfulness meditation, has also been shown to increase compassion for self and others. Following is a guided practice you can do.

Find a place to sit where you'll be comfortable. Begin by focusing on your breathing—not trying to change your breath but just noticing how it feels to breathe. Slowly, deeply, and comfortably, inhale and exhale.

As you focus on your breathing, allow yourself to connect with pleasurable feelings—feelings of kindness, friendliness, warmth, and compassion. These are the feelings you experience when you see a person you really care about; when your pet comes to greet you; when you do something nice for someone "just because." Recall that warmth and kindness you experience toward others; imagine those feelings right now, as though they were happening in this moment, and let yourself feel the joy, love, and other pleasurable feelings that come up for you. As you experience these feelings of kindness and compassion, gently say the following words:

May I be happy.
May I be healthy.
May I be peaceful.
May I be safe.

You can say these words in your head or out loud; either way, put feeling and meaning into them, and make sure that you really feel the words as you say them. If you have a hard time feeling kindness toward yourself, remember that habits take time to change—as best as you can, do not judge yourself or the exercise but just know that this is something you'll need to spend more time on.

Make sure that you practice this exercise regularly, and you will find yourself taking a more kind, loving, and compassionate attitude toward yourself.

Increasing Self-Compassion Through Self-Validation

It's not uncommon for people to dislike certain emotions and even judge themselves for feeling certain feelings; the problem with this is that it increases our emotional suffering. So, how do you change this habit of judging your emotions to be more self-compassionate? The first step is to increase your awareness. If you don't know how you think and feel about your emotions, you won't be able to change your response. Mindfulness, such as the mindfulness of emotions practice we did in chapter 1, will of course help with this. The next step is to start changing your self-talk. Here are three ways to validate your emotions (Van Dijk 2012).

1. Acknowledging. The most basic form of self-validating is acknowledging the presence of your emotion: for example, "I feel _____." By simply labeling the emotion (accurately!), you're validating it.
2. Allowing. Another form of self-validating is allowing yourself, or giving yourself permission, to feel the emotion, for example, "It's okay that I feel _____." You're not saying "It's okay" in the sense

that you like it or want it to hang around; you're just noting that you're allowed to feel it.

3. Understanding. The third and most difficult form of self-validating is saying, "It makes sense that I feel _____." You might be able to understand the emotion based on past experience (for example, "It makes sense that I feel anxious when I'm meeting new people, because I was bullied when I was a kid"), or based on the present (for example, "It makes sense that I feel anxious about public speaking, because it's not something I'm used to doing"). We can't always understand why we feel the way we do, but even if we can't understand our emotion, we can still validate it by either acknowledging its presence or allowing it.

Create Self-Validating Statements

Hopefully you've been able to identify which emotions you need to work on validating. If you've identified more than one emotion you judge yourself for feeling, choose just one to start with. You can always come back and work on the others later. In your journal, write out some statements to validate your emotion. Below are some examples to validate anger; feel free to use these if they resonate for you, or to tweak them to make them fit your emotion.

Emotion: Anger
- I feel angry.
- Anger is a normal human emotion that we all feel at times, so it's okay that I feel this way.
- I'm feeling angry; it's uncomfortable, but it is what it is.
- It makes sense that I'm feeling angry, because I just had a fight with my partner.
- I'm feeling angry right now, but that doesn't mean anything about me as a person.
- It makes sense that I have anger problems because of the environment I grew up in.

Chapter 5

TAKE REFUGE FROM YOUR PAIN

In this chapter, we're going to continue looking at skills that will help you to tolerate distress by learning skills to help you change your thinking. These skills usually take some practice when things are calm so that you'll be more able to draw on them when emotions become more intense, but in the long run, they'll provide you with more flexibility in managing your emotions. We'll start with a couple of acronyms to help you remember the skills and to put them all together; remember to add to your list of distress tolerance skills as you continue to learn new ways (or are reminded of ways you already knew!) of tolerating your distress.

REST

The acronym REST is a nice one to help you remember what to do when emotions start to intensify:

R—Relax

Take a deep breath. You may need to go even further than that and use some of your re-regulating skills such as paced breathing, tipping the temperature of your face with cold water, or doing a forward bend; and even then you may not feel *relaxed,* so don't worry! But the key here is to do something to help you calm yourself a little so you can get closer to your wise self. This will set the stage for the next step.

E—Evaluate

From your Wise Mind (see chapter 6 for more on this), ask yourself, *What am I worrying about? Am I in danger right now? What's the threat?* This helps us to put things in perspective a bit more; often when we can see what it is we're fearing will happen, we're able to see that it's not all that realistic, which can help to calm us further.

S—Set an intention

Ask yourself what skills you can use right now, then make a plan to use them. This is where that list you've been working on will come in handy by taking some of the thinking out of the equation for you—we all know how hard it can be to think straight when we're experiencing an intense emotion. Having your list means you don't have to think as hard, you just have to pull out your list and set an intention to use one of the skills you've already come up with.

T—Take action

The last step, of course, is to put your plan into action. Mindfully take the steps to use the skill.

Remember that these skills will be helpful no matter the painful emotion and no matter the behaviors you're dealing with—from struggling with your own emotions and the pain they cause to more problematic behaviors like substance use or avoidance through food, sleep, or self-harm.

RESISTT

The second acronym we'll use here is RESISTT (Van Dijk 2013), with the idea that, when an emotion arises and results in an urge, we want to resist acting on the urge! You're going to see many different examples of skills here, so remember to have your list of distress tolerance skills at hand to add to.

R: Reframe

We can learn to manage emotions more effectively by reframing, or changing, our perspective about something. You might be familiar with the sayings "making lemonade out of lemons" and "finding the silver lining in a situation;" both are examples of reframing—finding a positive in what seems to be negative, making problematic stuff more bearable. Keep in mind that reframing does not mean minimizing your pain or telling yourself you should "suck it up;" it's about trying to see another perspective. It's important to acknowledge the pain you're dealing with, and then work on changing your perspective.

There are many ways to reframe; here are a few techniques for you to try:

- You can compare yourself to someone else who isn't coping as well as you are. This isn't about minimizing your problems, nor is it about putting the other person down. Rather, it's about helping you see that even though things are difficult for you right now, they could also be worse (for example, *Things are hard right now, but my friend Kelly is in the hospital, so I can also see that things could be worse*).
- You can compare yourself now to a time in your life when you weren't coping as well (for example, *I'm really struggling right now, but this time last year I was still smoking weed to cope*).
- Or you could compare your own situation to a broader situation in the world (for

example, *Things are hard for me since I lost my job, but I'm grateful I have my family to help me through these difficult times, whereas others might not have this kind of support*).

The way we talk to ourselves about what's happening in our lives can change the way we think and feel about things. And unfortunately, it's a fairly common human experience to focus on the negative, or catastrophize, where we imagine the worst outcome imaginable. Changing your negative thoughts about a situation usually makes it more tolerable, and you'll be more likely to get through it without doing things that could make it worse. To help change your negative self-talk, write out some coping statements to use when you get into situations that trigger intense emotions. That way you'll be less likely to make the situation worse, and more likely to cope in effective ways instead of turning to target behaviors. Here are some examples of coping statements:

These feelings are painful, but I know I can bear them.

I can get through this.

This pain will not last forever.

If you can't think of more encouraging or neutral ways of talking to yourself, feel free to use the examples provided, if they resonate for you. You can also ask yourself what you would say to a loved one if they were in your shoes. How can you reframe to help yourself when things get difficult? Add your ideas to your distress tolerance skills list.

E: Engage in an Activity

Sometimes doing something that creates some kind of pleasurable emotion (such as peace, calm, satisfaction, or even enjoyment) is the best way to distract yourself from painful emotions. But remember, you don't have to wait until you feel overwhelmed by painful emotions in order to do one of these activities. It's also helpful to engage in these types of activities on a regular basis. In fact, you should try to do something pleasurable every day. Exercise is especially important because not only is it good for your overall physical health, but it's also been shown to be an effective treatment for depression in some cases (Babyak et al. 2000). Plus, exercise causes your body to release endorphins, which are the body's natural feel good chemicals that can trigger positive feelings, naturally boosting your mood.

Following is a list of over one hundred pleasurable activities you can use to distract yourself.

- Talk to a friend on the telephone.
- Go out and visit a friend.
- Invite a friend to come to your home.

- Text or email your friends.
- Organize a party.
- Exercise.
- Lift weights.
- Do yoga, tai chi, or Pilates, or take classes to learn.
- Stretch your muscles.
- Go for a long walk in a park or someplace else that's peaceful.
- Go outside and watch the clouds.
- Go for a jog.
- Ride your bike.
- Go for a swim.
- Go hiking.
- Do something exciting, like surfing, rock climbing, skiing, skydiving, motorcycle riding, or kayaking, or go learn how to do one of these things.
- Go to your local playground and join a game being played or watch a game.
- Go play something you can do by yourself if no one else is around, like basketball, bowling, handball, miniature golf, billiards, or hitting a tennis ball against the wall.
- Get a massage; this can also help soothe your emotions.
- Get out of your house, even if you just sit outside.

- Go for a drive in your car or go for a ride on public transportation.
- Plan a trip to a place you've never been before.
- Sleep or take a nap.
- Eat chocolate (it's good for you in moderation!) or eat something else you really like.
- Eat your favorite ice cream.
- Cook your favorite dish or meal.
- Cook a recipe that you've never tried before.
- Take a cooking class.
- Go out for something to eat.
- Go outside and play with your pet.
- Borrow a friend's dog and take it to the park.
- Give your pet a bath.
- Go outside and watch the birds and other animals.
- Watch a funny video on the internet.
- Watch a funny movie (start collecting funny movies to watch when you're feeling difficult emotions).
- Go to the movie theater and watch whatever's playing.
- Watch television.
- Listen to the radio.
- Go to a sporting event, like a baseball or football game.
- Play a game with a friend.

- Play solitaire.
- Play video games.
- Go online to chat.
- Visit your favorite websites.
- Create your own website.
- Create your own online blog.
- Join an online dating app.
- Sell something you no longer want on the internet.
- Buy something (within your budget).
- Do a puzzle with a lot of pieces.
- Go shopping.
- Go get a haircut.
- Go to a spa.
- Go to the library.
- Go to your favorite café for coffee or tea.
- Visit a museum or art gallery.
- Go to the mall or the park and watch other people; try to imagine what they're thinking.
- Pray.
- Meditate.
- Go to your church, synagogue, temple, or other place of worship.
- Join a group at your place of worship.
- Write a letter to God, the universe, or your higher power.
- Call a family member you haven't spoken to in a long time.
- Learn a new language.

- Sing or learn how to sing.
- Play a musical instrument or learn how to play one.
- Write a song.
- Listen to some upbeat, happy music (start collecting happy songs for times when you're feeling painful emotions).
- Turn on some loud music and dance.
- Memorize lines from your favorite movie, play, or song.
- Make a movie or video with your smartphone.
- Take photographs.
- Join a public-speaking group and write a speech.
- Participate in a local theater group.
- Sing in a local choir.
- Join a club.
- Plant a garden.
- Work outside.
- Knit, crochet, or sew—or learn how to.
- Make a scrapbook with pictures.
- Paint your nails.
- Change your hair color.
- Take a bubble bath or shower.
- Work on your car, truck, motorcycle, or bicycle.
- Sign up for a class that interests you at a local college, adult school, or online.

- Read your favorite book, magazine, paper, or poem.
- Read a celebrity magazine.
- Write a letter to a friend or family member.
- Finger paint.
- Write a poem, story, movie, or play about your life or someone else's life.
- Do a craft.
- Write a loving letter to yourself when you're feeling good and keep it with you to read when you're feeling distressed.
- Make a list of ten things you're good at or that you like about yourself when you're feeling good, and keep it with you to read when you're feeling painful emotions.
- Draw a picture.
- Paint a picture.
- Spend time with someone you care about, respect, or admire.
- Make a list of the people you admire and want to be like—it can be anyone real or fictional throughout history. Describe what you admire about these people.
- Write a story about the most outlandish, funniest, or most meaningful thing that has ever happened to you.
- Make a list of ten things you would like to do before you die.

- Make a list of ten celebrities you would like to be friends with and describe why.
- Make a list of ten celebrities you would like to date and describe why.
- Write a letter to someone who has made your life better and tell them why. (You don't have to send the letter if you don't want to.)
- Create your own list of pleasurable activities.

Here's an example of using pleasurable activities to distract yourself:

> *Karen was feeling lonely and had nothing to do. As she sat alone at home, she began to think about how lonely she'd been her whole life and how she was hurt by her father when she was growing up. Very quickly, Karen was overwhelmed with very painful emotions. In fact, the memories also triggered physical pain in her shoulder. Karen began to cry and didn't know what to do. Luckily, she remembered the distraction plan she had created. Exercise had always been a powerful tool for Karen, so she went for a long walk in the park while she listened to some of her favorite music. The activity didn't erase her memories or remove her pain completely, but the long walk did soothe her and prevent her from being overwhelmed with sadness.*

CHORES ARE ACTIVITIES!

Strangely, many people don't schedule enough time to take care of themselves or their living environments. As a result, tasks and chores go uncompleted. Here, then, is the perfect opportunity to do something to take care of yourself and your environment. The next time you're in a situation in which your emotions become too painful, temporarily distract yourself by engaging in one of the following activities. Add the ones you're willing to do, and any others you can think of, to your list:

Wash the dishes or load the dishwasher.

Make phone calls to people you haven't spoken to recently (but not someone you're angry with).

Clean your room or house, or go help a friend with their cleaning or gardening project.

Clean out your closet and donate your old clothes.

Redecorate a room or at least the walls.

Organize your books, music playlists, computer desktop, and so forth.

Make a plan for getting a job if you don't already have one, or make a plan for finding a better job.

Wash your car (or someone else's!).

Mow the lawn.

Clean your garage.

Wash the laundry.

Do your homework.

Do work that you've brought home from your job.

Polish your shoes.

Polish your jewelry.

Clean the bathtub and then take a bath.

Water your plants.

Pay the bills.

Go to a support meeting, like Narcotics Anonymous, Alcoholics Anonymous, or Overeaters Anonymous.

Here's an example of using tasks and chores to distract yourself:

Mike was stressed about his job; on his way home from work he drove past the liquor store and on a whim he stopped and bought himself a bottle. It was only after he had taken his second drink that he realized he had just lost his three months of sobriety; shame immediately arose and Mike didn't know what to do. Quickly, he began to feel light-headed and confused, and his emotions became very intense. But this time, instead of taking another drink and making more choices that he would regret later, he opened his wallet and pulled out the distraction plan he had made. He had written down, "Take a REST and distract with chores." So he took a few breaths to relax and then evaluated the situation. He recognized that he was feeling shame—but was not in danger. Next, he set an intention to go see his parents. A visit would take him at least two hours, and connecting with his parents would help him feel less shame since they understood what he was going through. And finally, he took action by walking a half mile to his parents' home. Getting out of his house helped soothe his intense emotions, and he was able to have his father come home with him to ensure he poured out what was left of the alcohol.

S: Someone Else

Another great way to distract yourself from pain is to divert your attention to someone else.

Here are some examples. Add the ones you're willing to do, and any others that you can think of, to your list of skills:

- **Do something for someone else.** Call your friends and ask if they need help doing something, such as a chore or running an errand. Ask your parents, grandparents, or siblings if you can help them with something. Tell them you're feeling bored and you're looking for something to do. Call up someone you know and offer to take them out to lunch. Find a charity to donate a sum of money that is reasonable for you. If you can plan ahead for moments like these when you're overwhelmed with pain, call your local soup kitchen, homeless shelter, or volunteer organization. Plan to participate in activities that help other people. Join a local political activities group, environmental group, or other organization, and get involved in helping other people.
- **Take your attention off yourself.** Go to a local store, shopping center, bookstore, or park. Just sit and watch other people or walk around among them. Watch what they do. Observe how they dress. Listen to their conversations. Count the number of buttons they're wearing on their shirts. Observe as many details about these other people as you

can. Count the number of people with blond hair versus the number of people with brown, red, and gray hair. When your thoughts return to your pain, refocus on the details of the people you're watching.

- **Think of someone you care about.** Keep a picture of this person on your phone, or in your wallet or purse. This could be your partner, your parent, children, or friend, or it could be someone else you admire, such as Mother Teresa, Gandhi, Jesus, the Dalai Lama, and so on. It could even be a movie star, an athlete, or someone you've never met. Then, when you're feeling distressed, take out the picture and imagine a healing, peaceful conversation you would have with that person if you could talk to them at that moment when you're feeling distressed. What would they say to you that would help make you feel better? Imagine them saying those words to you.

Here's an example of distracting yourself by paying attention to someone else:

> *Watching the evening news, Louis found himself feeling very distressed by all of the pain he was seeing in the world around him—the wars; the environmental disasters; homelessness; people who were suffering with mental illness, physical illness, and addictions. It felt like everywhere he looked all he saw was suffering.*

Very quickly, Louis became overwhelmed by sadness, anger and fear. Recognizing that his emotions were intensifying and becoming more difficult to bear, Louis went to his desk, where he kept a picture of his mother. He sat down and started to talk to his mother as if she were there with him. He asked for strength and guidance to handle the pain he was feeling. Then he imagined what she would say to him, and he started to feel better. Later, when he was able to think more clearly, he returned to what he needed to do that day.

I: Intense Sensations

Generating intense physical sensations can sometimes distract us from painful emotions. What physical sensations might take your mind off your emotions? For example, if you turn to self-harm to deal with painful emotions, try holding an ice cube in your hand (Linehan 2003); this causes an intense sensation but doesn't come with the negative consequences of self-harm. Here are some other things you might try:

Take a hot or cold bath or shower (keep in mind that the cold water, if you can go that route, will also help by activating your parasympathetic nervous system!), or go for a walk in cold or hot weather.

Snap a rubber band on your wrist.

Chew on crushed ice or frozen fruit.

Do some stretches.
Have (healthy) sex.
Eat something sour (like a sour key or a lime).

S: Shut It Out

Quite often, physically leaving a situation and going somewhere calm and quiet will make it more likely that you can use your skills and manage emotions more effectively. Sometimes, of course, this isn't enough, and you may find yourself continuing to dwell on the problem even after you've physically left the situation. This is when shutting it out—the DBT skill known as *pushing away* (Linehan 2014)—can be helpful. With this skill, you use your imagination to convince your mind that the problem isn't something that can be worked on now, and that it needs to be put away for the time being.

The first step to shutting it out is to write out the problem (or list of problems, if there's more than one) contributing to your emotional pain. Next, ask yourself if this is a problem you can solve right now: Do you have the skills to solve the problem? Is there a solution to the problem that you can start working on in this very moment?

If you see that you can solve the problem, then stop right here and solve it! Shutting it out is only effective if you can convince your mind that you can't do anything about the current problem right now.

For a problem you can't solve, close your eyes and get a sense of something that represents it. For example, if you had an argument with your boss, you might conjure an image of your boss, or visualize their name. (If you can't visualize very well, see if you can get a sense of the problem in some way, or feel it.) Next, imagine yourself placing that representation of your problem in a box, putting a lid on the box, and tying the lid on with string or rope—or chains! The goal here is to convince your mind that the problem can't be worked on now and must be put away for the time being, so do what you have to do to shut it out. For example, you might need to imagine putting the box on a shelf in a closet, shutting the closet door, and putting a padlock on the door.

You can also make this technique more concrete:

- Take the problem you've written down on a piece of paper and literally put it away.
- Tell a worry doll about the problem before you go to sleep. A worry doll is a doll that is put under the pillow and will take over the worrying for the person, allowing them to sleep better rather than lie awake worrying.
- Put the problem in a "God box," a container with an opening on top. When using a God

box, you write your problem, worry, or difficult decision on a piece of paper and put it in the box, turning the matter over to God (or higher power, or whatever version of this fits for you).

If you shut the problem out in some way already, fantastic; add your method to your distress tolerance skills list. If this concept is new to you, write out some ideas you'd be willing to try. Keep in mind that this skill, and any other approach that involves avoiding thinking certain thoughts or feelings, can be helpful for some people, but pushing thoughts and emotions away often makes them stronger, so this skill should be used sparingly. When you're in a more regulated state and feel like you have the skills, you can also start to take things out of your container and work on problem solving.

T: Think Neutral Thoughts

The human brain is a wonderful thought-producing machine. It turns out millions of thoughts every day. Most of the time, this makes our lives much easier. But unfortunately, we can't fully control what our brain thinks about. Here's an example:

Imagine a picture of your favorite cartoon character, such as Bugs Bunny, Snoopy, Superman, or whoever. Close your eyes and see the character in vivid detail in your mind's eye.

Remember exactly what it looks like. Think about the character for about fifteen seconds. Got it? Now, for the next thirty seconds, do your best not to think about that character. Try to block them from your thoughts. But be honest with yourself and notice how often they pop into your thoughts.

It's impossible not to think about them; and in fact, the harder you try not to think about that character, the more power you give to the image and the more your brain keeps bringing it into your thoughts. It's almost as if the harder you try to forget something, the harder your brain tries to remember it. This is why forcing yourself to forget about something that happened to you is impossible. It's also why you can't simply force yourself to get rid of emotions that you don't want.

So, instead of trying to force yourself to forget something—a memory, thought, or something else that's uncomfortable or painful—try to distract your thoughts with other memories or creative images. Here are some examples. Add the ones you're willing to do, and any others you can think of, to your list:

- Remember events from your past that were pleasant, fun, or exciting. Try to remember as many details as possible about these happy memories. What did you do? Who were you with? What happened?

- Look outside at the natural world around you. Observe the flowers, trees, sky, and landscape as closely as you can. Observe any animals that are around. Listen to the sounds that they make. Or if you live in a city without much nature around you, either do your best to observe what you can, or close your eyes and imagine a scene you've observed in the past.
- Imagine yourself as an avenger correcting some past or future event in your life. How would you do it? What would people say to you?
- Imagine yourself getting praise from someone whose opinion matters to you. What did you do? What does this person say to you? Why does this person's opinion matter to you?
- Imagine your wildest fantasy coming true. What would it be? Who else would be involved? What would you do afterward?
- Keep a copy of a favorite prayer, poem, or saying with you. Then, when you feel distressed, pull it out and read it to yourself. Imagine the words calming and soothing you. Use imagery (such as a light coming down from Heaven or the universe) that soothes you as you read the words.

- Count (for example, count your inhalations as you do paced breathing, or count backward from one hundred by threes).
- Say a prayer or repeat a mantra that you find comforting, such as "It is what it is" or "Peace and calm."
- Sing your favorite song or recite a nursery rhyme or poem.

Here's an example of distracting with neutral thoughts:

Joel struggled to manage his anger. When he found himself feeling angry, he noticed that he would often rehash the situation that was triggering him, going over and over it in his mind. He didn't know what to do to get his mind unstuck; he would often find himself screaming at his friends or whoever else was around.

But after creating a distraction plan, Joel thought of other ideas. The next time he noticed the feeling of anger arising, he remembered to use his REST strategy. First, he did his best to relax by taking a few slow breaths. Then, he evaluated the situation and realized he wasn't in any danger. Next, he set an intention to distract his thoughts, so he took action and went to his bedroom to lie down. Then, he started to use neutral thoughts to distract himself. He began counting his breaths as he did paced breathing; and he repeated the mantra he had come up with: I can manage, I can feel calmer. This gradually helped Joel to reduce the intensity of his anger, and he was able to turn to his list of distress tolerance skills to find something else to prevent the anger from overwhelming him.

T: Take a Break

Sometimes the best thing that you can do is leave. If you're in a very painful situation with someone and you recognize that your emotions are going to overwhelm you and possibly make the situation worse than it is already, then often it's best to just leave. Remember, if you're already overwhelmed by your emotions, it will be harder for you to think of a healthy resolution to your problem. Maybe it's best to put some distance between you and the situation in order to give yourself time to calm your emotions and consider what to do next. Just walk away if that's the best you can do. It will be better than adding fuel to the emotional fire.

Here's an example of leaving to distract yourself:

Anna was in a large department store shopping for a blouse. She wanted one of the clerks to help her find her size, but the store clerk was busy with other customers. Anna waited as long as she could and kept trying to get the clerk's attention, but nothing worked. Anna recognized that she was getting angry very quickly. She was ready to tear the blouse in half. She didn't know what else to do. In the past, she would have stayed in the store and gotten angrier, but this time she remembered to leave. She walked out of the store, did some shopping elsewhere, and returned to get the blouse later, when the store was less crowded and when she was feeling more in control of her behaviors.

Take a Vacation

We all need to relax in order to refresh our bodies, minds, and spirits. Yet many people don't take time out for themselves because they feel like they'd be disappointing someone else, like their boss, spouse, family, or friends. Or, they might feel guilty or ashamed for doing anything for themselves. Others might struggle with the constant need to please others, and as a result, they neglect to take care of themselves. But people who don't take care of themselves lead very unbalanced lives.

How long can you continue to take care of someone else without taking care of yourself? Imagine a woman who stands on a street corner on a hot summer day holding a jug of cold water. She pours drinks for every pedestrian who walks by and, of course, everyone is grateful. But what happens when she's thirsty and goes to get a drink? The woman spent a long day helping everyone else and neglecting herself, and the jug is now empty. How often do you feel like this woman? How often do you run out of time for yourself because you've spent all of it taking care of other people? Helping others is a good thing to do as long as it doesn't come at too much of an expense of your own physical or mental health. You need to take care of yourself, and that doesn't mean you're selfish; it's *self-care*.

Here are some ideas you can use to take a vacation from stress. Add the ones you're willing to do, and any other ideas you can think of, to your list:

- Treat yourself as kindly as you treat other people. Do one nice thing for yourself that you've been putting off.
- Devote time to yourself, even if it's just a few hours during the week, by doing things like taking a walk or preparing your favorite meal.
- Take a half day off from work. Go someplace beautiful, like a park, the ocean, a lake, the mountains, a museum, or even someplace like a shopping center.
- Take time to do things for your own life, like shopping, errands, doctor's appointments, and so on.

Peaceful Place Visualization

Peaceful place visualization is a powerful stress-reduction technique. Using it, you can soothe yourself by imagining a peaceful place to help you feel more relaxed and to manage your emotions more effectively. The truth is, your brain and body often can't tell the difference between what's really happening to you and what you're just imagining. So if you can successfully create a peaceful, relaxing scene in your thoughts, your body will often respond to those soothing ideas.

Make sure you conduct this exercise in a quiet room where you'll be free from distractions. Allow yourself the time and the freedom to relax. You deserve it.

Before beginning this exercise, think of a real or imaginary place that makes you feel peacful, secure, calm, or relaxed. It can be an indoor or an outdoor space. It can be a real place that you've visited in the past, such as the beach, a park, a field, a place of worship, a room in your home, and so on. Or it can be a place that you've imagined, such as a white cloud floating in the sky, a medieval castle, or the surface of the moon. It can be anywhere. It's also important that there are no other people in your peaceful place, since we can't control other people, even in our own imagination. Pets or other animals can be there if you wish, but no people allowed! If you have trouble thinking of a place, think of a color that makes you feel relaxed or calm, such as pink or baby blue. Just do your best. In the exercise, you'll be guided through exploring this place in more detail. But before you begin, make sure you already have a place in mind, and remember—thinking of it should make you feel peaceful and relaxed.

Complete the following sentences about your peaceful place in your journal before beginning the visualization:
- My peaceful place is _____.
- My peaceful place makes me feel _____.

To begin, sit in a comfortable chair with your feet and hands resting comfortably. Close your eyes. Take a slow, long breath in through your nose. Feel your belly expand like a balloon as you breathe in. Hold it for five seconds: 1, 2, 3, 4, 5. Then, release it slowly through your mouth. Feel your belly collapse like a balloon losing its air. Again, take a slow, long breath in through your nose and feel your stomach expand. Hold it for five seconds: 1, 2, 3, 4, 5. Then, exhale slowly through your mouth. One more time: Take a slow, long breath in through your nose and feel your stomach expand. Hold it for five seconds: 1, 2, 3, 4, 5. Then, exhale slowly through your mouth. Now, begin to take slow, long breaths without holding them, and continue to breathe smoothly for the rest of this exercise.

Now, with your eyes closed, imagine that you enter your peaceful place, using all of your senses to ground yourself in the scene.

First, look around using your imaginary sense of sight. What does this place look like? Is it daytime or nighttime? Is it sunny or cloudy? Notice the details. Are you alone or are there other animals there with you? What are they doing? If you're outside, look up and notice the sky. Look out at the horizon. If you're inside, notice what the walls and the furniture look like. Is the room light or dark? Choose something soothing to look at. Then, continue looking for a few moments using your imaginary sense of sight.

Next, use your imaginary sense of hearing. What do you hear? Do you hear music? Do you hear the wind or the ocean? Do you hear the sound of animals or nature? Choose something soothing to hear. Then, listen for a few moments using your imaginary sense of hearing.

Now, use your imaginary sense of smell. If you're inside, what does it smell like? Does it smell fresh? Do you have a fire burning that you can smell? Or, if you're outside, can you smell the air, the grass, the ocean, or the flowers? Choose to smell something soothing in your scene. Then, take a few moments to use your imaginary sense of smell.

Next, notice if you can feel anything with your imaginary sense of touch. What are you sitting or standing on in your scene?

Can you feel the wind? Can you feel something you're touching in the scene? Choose to touch something soothing in your scene. Then, take a few moments to use your imaginary sense of touch.

Last, use your imaginary sense of taste. Are you eating or drinking anything in this scene? Choose something soothing to taste. Then, take a few moments to use your imaginary sense of taste.

Now, take a few more moments to explore your safe place using all of your imaginary senses. Do your best to let this experience really sink in as much as possible, feeling its calm, healing properties.

Now, let's practice using this skill to regulate emotions.

Just for a moment, set aside this peaceful place you've envisioned around yourself, think of a recent troubling situation—something that caused you to feel irritated, annoyed, or stressed, for example. On a scale from 0 (no emotion) to 10 (most intense emotion imaginable), the feeling should be around a 3 or 4. Imagine that situation now as best as you can so that you actually experience the emotion. Once you feel it, go back to your peaceful place. Picture it in your mind, feel it with all of your senses once again, really letting yourself be there, allowing yourself to experience the calm, peace, and security of that place. Stay with that peaceful experience as long as you'd like, and see if you can get those emotions back down to a 1 or even 0.

Remember that you can come back to this place in your imagination whenever you need to feel peaceful and relaxed. You can also come back whenever you're feeling sad, angry, restless, or in pain. Look around one last time to remember what it looks like. Now, keep your eyes closed and return your focus to your breathing. Again, take some slow, long breaths in through your nose and exhale through your mouth. Then, when you feel ready, open your eyes and return your focus to the room.

Hopefully you saw your emotions come back down. And don't forget that you can use other skills in conjunction with the peaceful place, as well. For example, if your emotion is intense, you might need to do some re-regulating with skills like the forward bend or deep breathing before you can use your peaceful place; or, if you're using your peaceful place to re-regulate and you find that the emotions don't quite come down to a 0, you can also use more skills you've been learning in this book to reduce the emotion further. This peaceful place is one more tool to help you tolerate your distress more effectively.

Chapter 6
ACCEPT AND MOVE BEYOND

The distress tolerance skills we've been looking at so far in this book have mostly been skills that will help you to tolerate distressing or uncomfortable emotions in the short term. In this chapter, we'll be looking at some skills that will help you in the longer term: first, through finding connection—with a higher power, with yourself, and with others. We'll do some practices to help you discover that connection for yourself; or, if this is something you're already connected to, you'll learn ways of deepening that connection, and drawing on it in a more conscious way when you need it.

The second skill we'll look at in this chapter is radical acceptance: acknowledging reality as it actually is. You'll learn how each of these skills can be helpful when it comes to learning to tolerate distress. You'll also have the opportunity to consider how you may have used these skills already in your life—as well as how they can help you tolerate distress moving forward—and you'll be encouraged to engage in some exercises to help you practice each of them. Remember these skills take longer to develop and will likely take work and energy, so do your best to keep an open mind and be patient with yourself.

Connect to Higher Power

Whether you believe in one God, many gods, a divine universe, or the goodness that exists within each human being, having faith in something bigger and more powerful than yourself can often make *you* feel empowered, safe, and calm. This is what people mean when they talk about believing in a "higher power" or seeing "the big picture" in life. Believing in something divine, holy, or special can help you endure stressful situations as well as help you soothe yourself.

At some point in life, we all feel hopeless or powerless. We've all experienced unfortunate situations during which we felt alone and needed strength. Sometimes unexpected circumstances hurt us or the people we care about. These situations might include being the victim of a crime, experiencing a natural disaster, getting into an accident, having someone close to us die, or being diagnosed with a serious illness. Having faith in something special during times like these can often help you feel connected to a bigger purpose in life. And remember, your faith doesn't have to involve God if that's not what you believe in. Some people only put their faith in the goodness of the people they love. Yet basic beliefs like these are often powerful enough to help people find the strength and comfort to lead happy, healthy lives.

While you're exploring your spirituality, remember that your beliefs can change over time. Sometimes a person is raised in a religious or spiritual tradition that no longer makes sense or feels helpful to them. Yet, despite these feelings, a person will sometimes continue to attend the services of that tradition out of a sense of obligation. The truth is, if your spiritual tradition is no longer giving you peace and strength, it's okay (and even important!) to reexamine that faith and to make changes.

Connect to Your Higher Power

Use the following questions to help you consider your beliefs and some ways in which you can strengthen and use those beliefs on a regular basis. Spend some time responding to these questions in your journal.

What are some of your beliefs about a higher power or a big picture that give you strength and comfort?

Why are these beliefs important to you?

How do these beliefs make you feel?

How do these beliefs make you think about others?

How do these beliefs make you think about life in general?

How do you acknowledge your beliefs throughout your daily life? (For example, do you go to church, synagogue, or temple? Do you pray? Do you meditate? Do you talk to other people about your beliefs? Do you read books about your beliefs? Do you help other people?)

What else would you be willing to do in order to strengthen your beliefs?

What can you do to remind yourself of your beliefs on a regular basis?

What can you say or do to remind yourself of your beliefs the next time you're feeling distressed?

Higher-Power Activities

Here are some additional activities to help you feel more connected to your higher power, the universe, and the big picture. Add the ones you're willing to do to your list of distress tolerance skills:

- **If you do believe in the teachings of a particular religion or faith, find related activities that make you feel more empowered and calmer.** Go to your church, synagogue, or temple for services. Talk to the person who runs your services. Talk to other members of your faith about how they've handled difficult experiences. Join discussion groups formed at your place of worship. Read the books that are important to your faith. Find passages that give you strength, and mark them or copy them to keep with you in your wallet, your purse, or on your phone so you can read them no matter where you are.
- **Remember that your higher power can also be something other than God.** Your higher power can be a person who makes you feel stronger and more confident to deal with the challenges that you face. Think of someone you admire who can be your higher power. Describe that person. What makes them special? Then, the next time you're in a difficult or distressing situation, act as if you are that person, and notice how you handle the situation differently.

- **Look up at the stars.** The light you're seeing is thousands of years old, and it has traveled from stars that are billions of miles away. In fact, each time you look up at the stars, you're looking through a time machine and seeing the universe as it looked thousands of years ago. Strangely, some of the stars you're looking may have already died, but their light is just reaching your eyes on the Earth. Look up at the stars and recognize that whatever created them also created you, whether it was God or a cosmic force.
- **You are connected to the stars.** Imagine yourself connecting with the universe. Sit in a comfortable chair, close your eyes, and imagine a beam of light shining down from the universe. Like a laser beam, the light shines on the top of your head and fills you with a feeling of peace. Now, imagine the light spreading all over your body, relaxing every muscle. Now, imagine your legs stretching down through the floor like giant tree roots, going all the way down into the center of the Earth. Imagine these roots tapping into the energy that drives the planet. Feel your body fill with confidence as your legs absorb the golden energy flowing up from the Earth.

- **Think about our planet Earth.** Water is the most important substance for sustaining life on our planet. Yet if we were much closer to the sun, all the water on our planet would evaporate because the temperature would be too hot, and if we were much farther away, all the water would freeze because the temperature would be too cold. Somehow, we were lucky enough to be in just the right place for life to form. Even if you don't believe in a religious purpose, ask yourself what it means that you live on a planet with just the right climate and elements for life to exist. How did this happen, and what does it mean about your life?
- **Go to the beach.** Try to count the grains in a handful of sand. Now, try to imagine how many handfuls of sand there are in the world, on all the beaches and in all the deserts. Try to imagine how many billions of years must have passed to create so many grains of sand. And again, recognize that the chemical elements that make up the sand also exist in you. Stand with your feet in the sand and imagine feeling connected to the planet.
- **Go to a park or to a field and observe the trees, the grass, and the animals.** Again, recognize that whatever created all of that also created you. Remember that all living

things are made of the same chemical elements. On a subatomic scale, there isn't much difference between you and many other life forms. Yet you are still different and special. What is it that makes you unique?

- **Think about the human body, especially your own.** Each human being is more wonderful than a piece of artwork and more complex than any computer ever invented. Everything about you is largely determined by your DNA, the instructions that are found in every cell of your body. Yet amazingly, each set of instructions that creates every part of your body is composed of just four chemical elements that are repeated in different combinations. These different combinations are called genes, and these are the instructions you inherit from your parents that make up the spectrum of your possible physical and biological traits such as your eye color and the structure of your heart. Incredibly, it only takes an estimated twenty thousand genes to design a human being (according to Carl Zimmer's article "Scientists Finish the Human Genome at Last" in *The New York Times,* published July 23, 2021). Imagine trying to write so few instructions in order to create a body that thinks, breathes, eats, moves, and does everything else you do.

Plus, remember that this same number of instructions is also responsible for creating approximately eighty-six billion neurons in your brain, sixty thousand miles(!) of blood vessels throughout your body, six hundred skeletal muscles, two hundred bones, thirty-two teeth, and ten pints of blood.

Some people might prefer to simply believe in their own internal wisdom. We all have internal wisdom, although sometimes it can be more difficult to access than at others, and for some people, tapping into it takes more practice. If you would prefer to connect to your own internal higher power, or if you'd like to strengthen this connection in addition to that with your higher power, practicing getting to your Wise Mind can be very helpful.

Getting to Your Wise Mind

Acting from our Wise Mind means finding a balance between our emotions and our reasoning and following our intuition, or gut instinct, about what's in our best interest in the long run (Linehan 2014). Wise Mind has us considering how we feel (as well as our logical thoughts about a situation), weighing the possible consequences of different actions we might choose, and considering our values. With our Wise Mind, we base our decisions or behavior on all of these things. In other words, when we're acting from our Wise Mind, we're *choosing* how we want to act rather than simply *reacting*.

Like any new skill, it can be difficult to access that internal wisdom, especially when you're facing overwhelming emotions. The human tendency is to fall back into old habits and patterns. Here are some ideas to help improve your ability to access your Wise Mind; give each a try (or come up with your own), find one that resonates with you, and practice it as often as you can so that getting to your Wise Mind starts to come more naturally, providing emotional relief when things are getting tense.

Mindfulness. The "mindfulness of emotions" practice from chapter 1 is a good place to start for learning to notice your emotions, thoughts, physical sensations, and urges. Over time you'll learn to just observe these internal experiences rather than react to them. Of course, you don't have to do just this particular practice; any mindfulness practice will help you with this noticing, so be sure to incorporate mindfulness into your daily routine.

Self-talk. How you talk to yourself can influence how you think and feel about things. Bring to mind a recent situation that was painful for you. As you notice the emotion arising within you, focus on saying things to yourself that you would say to your best friend (or partner, or even a pet) if they were feeling this way: "It's okay that you feel like this. You've felt like this before, and you know it doesn't last forever.

You'll get through this." Talking to yourself as you would a friend can reduce the pain you're feeling and help you get to your Wise Mind.

Ask your Wise Mind. Ask yourself, *What does my Wise Mind say right now?* Then, listen quietly and see if you get an answer. You might want to close your eyes to do this.

Breathe. Do a breathing practice you like to get to your Wise Mind. You might also pair this with a mantra or saying, such as "Get to" (on the inhale) "Wise Mind" (on the exhale). Make it fit for you.

Taking On an Attitude of Gratitude

Let's look at how you can use a gratitude practice to strengthen your connection to yourself, your higher power, or to others when you're feeling distressing or painful emotions. It can be challenging to feel thankful while in a crisis, but gratitude can help us manage our emotions effectively to get through difficult, emotionally charged times.

Before employing this skill, you might first need to turn to one of the fast-acting skills (like the forward bend, a breathing practice, and so on) we covered in chapter 2 to get your emotions somewhat regulated. Over time you'll likely need these skills less often as you turn to other skills that help you prevent emotions from getting really intense in the first place; but until that's the case, be sure to use whatever skills you need to prevent yourself from making a situation even more difficult.

Once you've reduced the intensity of the emotion (or if you were able to catch it before it became intense), focus on something you feel grateful for. It might be someone in your life now or from your past, your job, the roof over your head, the country you live in, and so forth. *(When I'm feeling angry at the most recent problem life has sent my way, I hear myself thinking, First-world problems. I don't mean this in a self-judgmental way, but rather as a reminder that I have so many things to be grateful for—things I might not have, had I been born in another part of the world.)*

The key with this practice, of course, is finding what works for you. It's important to make sure you're not invalidating your experience—rather, you're reminding yourself of what you can be grateful for, turning your attention to those people or things, instead of staying focused on the problem. You might find it helpful to combine this skill with other skills, such as taking an open posture, putting on a half-smile, distracting yourself from the problem, or doing a breathing practice. In fact, it's always important to not forget to breathe!

So far in this chapter we've been looking at how to foster connection: with our higher power, with others, and within ourselves. Now we'll move to a different but related skill: radical acceptance.

Radical Acceptance

In DBT, the word "dialectic" means to balance and compare two things that appear very different or even contradictory. One of the primary dialectics we work with is between change and acceptance (Linehan 1993). You need to change the behaviors in your life that are creating more suffering for yourself and others while simultaneously also accepting yourself the way you are. This might sound contradictory, but it's a key part of this treatment. DBT focuses on acceptance *and* change, not acceptance *or* change.

Radical acceptance is one of the hardest skills to practice because it will require you to look at yourself and the world in a different way. However, it's also one of the most important (Linehan 1993). *Radical acceptance* means that you accept something completely, without judging it. For example, radically accepting the present moment means that you don't fight it, get angry at it, or try to change it into something that it's not. To radically accept the present moment means that you must acknowledge that the present moment is what it is due to a long chain of events and decisions made by you and other people *in the past*. The present moment never spontaneously leaps into existence without having been caused by events that already took place. Imagine that each moment of your life is connected like a line of dominoes that knock each other down.

But remember, radically accepting something doesn't mean that you give up and simply accept every painful situation that happens to you. Some situations in life are unjust, such as when someone abuses or assaults you. But for other situations in life, you share at least some responsibility. There's a balance between what you created and what others have created. However, many people struggling with overwhelming emotions often feel like life just "happens" to them, not recognizing their own role in creating a situation. As a result, their first reaction is to get angry. In fact, a client once said that anger was her "default emotion," meaning that when she was just being herself, she was angry. Her excessive hostility caused her to hurt herself—by drinking heavily, cutting herself, and constantly berating herself—and it also led to her hurting the people she cared about by constantly arguing with them.

In contrast, radically accepting the present moment opens up the opportunity for you to recognize the role that you have played in creating your current situation. And, as a result, it also creates an opportunity to respond to that situation in a new way that's less painful for yourself and others. In many ways, radical acceptance is like the Serenity Prayer, which says, "Grant me the serenity to accept the things I cannot change, the courage to change the things

I can, and the wisdom to know the difference." In the exercise below, you will find some questions to ask yourself when you want to use radical acceptance. But first, let's look at an example of how radical acceptance can help a person in a distressing situation.

Using Radical Acceptance

Christine and her boyfriend, John, had a difficult relationship. John spent a lot of his free time at the bar drinking with his friends, and, in response, Christine would get mad, threaten to leave him, and then do something destructive to "piss him off." This occurred regularly for five years. One night, Christine came home from work angry, and when John wasn't around to talk to, she suddenly felt hopeless about their relationship. So she called John to tell him that she was going to kill herself because she couldn't put up with his behavior any longer. John raced home to find Christine swallowing a handful of pills, and he made her spit them out. Then, he made her promise that she wouldn't do it again. She promised, and John went back to the bar, taking the keys to Christine's car so that she couldn't go anywhere. Now Christine got even angrier and called the police to report that her keys had been stolen. She walked up to the bar, found John's car, and smashed his windshield with a brick. She would have broken the other windows too, but *the police stopped her and arrested her. Needless to say, neither Christine nor John gave any consideration to using radical acceptance in this situation. Both of them were angry at each other, and by acting on their anger, they both ended up hurting themselves and one another.*

So how could this situation have occurred differently if Christine and John had practiced radical acceptance?

Let's consider the situation from Christine's point of view. Instead of threatening to kill herself, maybe she could have used the REST strategy and one of her distress tolerance skills. Remembering that the strategy for dealing with distressing situations is to relax, evaluate, set an intention, and take action, Christine could have (1) stopped what she was doing and taken a few breaths to relax (or at least to reduce the intensity of her emotions), (2) evaluated the situation and recognized that she was very emotional, (3) set an intention to use a distress tolerance skill to help her reduce the intensity of the emotions, and then (4) taken action by screaming into a pillow and going outside for a long walk. Or she could have called one of her friends to talk for a while (distracting herself, though, rather than venting about the situation and continuing to keep the emotions going!). After she'd cooled off a bit, Christine could have asked herself some questions and used radical acceptance to reexamine her situation. Let's look at this situation and see how it could have been handled a bit differently.

- *What events led up to Christine's situation?* She and John had been behaving and fighting like this for years. This night was nothing new. But she had come home angry about work, and she became even angrier with John because he wasn't around.
- *What role did Christine play in creating this situation?* Instead of trying to cope with her anger and frustration in a healthy way, she took her emotions out on herself and John. Also, Christine had had many reasons and opportunities in the past to try to change, or even end this problematic relationship if she wanted to, but she had chosen to stay.
- *What role did John play in creating this situation?* John had an alcohol problem that had been interfering with their relationship for five years. This night, he also didn't take the time to discuss Christine's suicidal behaviors with her. Instead, he chose to return to the bar, which made her even angrier.
- *What does Christine have control of in this situation?* She can end the relationship if she wants to; she can talk to John about seeking help to make healthy changes in their relationship; or she can choose a different way to cope with this distressing situation.

- *What doesn't Christine have control of in this situation?* Ultimately, it is John who has to seek help to stop his alcohol addiction. Christine can't make him stop drinking. She also doesn't have control of how John chooses to behave toward her in this situation.
- *What was Christine's response to this situation?* She tried to kill herself, and then she smashed John's windshield.
- *How did her response affect her own thoughts and feelings?* Her actions made her feel worse about herself and her relationship, and she kept thinking about why she was still in this destructive relationship.
- *How did her response affect the thoughts and feelings of other people?* Christine was arrested, which made both of them feel worse than they already did about themselves and their relationship.
- *How could Christine have changed her response to this situation so that it led to less suffering for her and John?* She could have used the REST strategy and other distress tolerance skills to cope with her pain and anger. She could also have used radical acceptance to reevaluate the situation so that she could choose to act in a different way. And perhaps she could even have chosen to give herself

some space—for instance, going to stay with a friend.

- *How could the situation have occurred differently if Christine had decided to radically accept the situation?* If Christine had been able to accept the reality as it was—including the causes that had led up to the situation—she likely would have experienced less emotional suffering. Radical acceptance would have allowed her to access her Wise Mind. Perhaps she could have made healthier choices, such as using distress tolerance skills or delaying talking to John to the next morning because neither of them was in the state of mind to have a helpful conversation. Or perhaps if Christine had ended the relationship, she could have made space in her life for a healthier relationship or simply spared herself the reoccurring pain of a destructive relationship.

Radical Acceptance

Think of a distressing situation that you experienced recently. Then, in your journal, answer these questions that will help you radically accept the situation:
- What happened in this distressing situation?
- What past events led up to this situation?
- What role did you play in creating this situation?

- What roles did other people play in creating this situation?
- What *do* you have control of in this situation?
- What *don't* you have control of in this situation?
- What was your response to this situation?
- How did your response affect your own thoughts, feelings, and behaviors?
- How did your response affect the thoughts, feelings and behaviors of other people?
- How could you have changed your response to this situation so that it led to less suffering for yourself and others?
- How could the situation have occurred differently if you had decided to radically accept the situation?

It's important to remember that radical acceptance also applies to accepting yourself. In this case, radical acceptance means embracing who you are without judging or criticizing yourself. Or, to put it another way, radically accepting yourself means loving yourself just the way you are, with all of your goodness and all of your faults. Finding the goodness inside of yourself might be a difficult challenge, especially if you're struggling with overwhelming emotions. Many people with this problem often think of themselves as being defective, bad, or unlovable. As a result, they overlook their positive qualities and add more pain to their lives. Accepting yourself as you are instead (remember, this doesn't mean that you stop trying to make changes!) will reduce the amount of suffering you experience.

CONCLUSION

One of the certainties of life is that it will involve pain—there's something we need to radically accept! Being able to tolerate distress—managing emotional pain and getting through crisis situations without making them worse by engaging in problematic or self-destructive behaviors—is one of the first steps to managing emotions more effectively, and to building a life worth living (Linehan 1993).

The aim of this book has been to bring distress tolerance skills into one place for you and help you expand your toolbox of skills to turn to when emotions start to become problematic. Remember that reading this book is just the start; hopefully you've been trying out the exercises we've included, finding the ones that resonate most for you, and adding them to your list of distress tolerance skills. As with any new skill, these will take practice, but over time you'll find that they will start to come more naturally to you.

Write a Letter to Yourself

In this last chapter, we're going to suggest one more skill that will help you put what you've learned together, by writing a letter to your future self. It's called a "Letter to Your Unwell Self," but please use the language that works best for you. Consider the timing of writing this letter—you may need to wait a bit until you get to that "better" place in order to do this. When you're ready, you can use the following questions to help you consider what you might want to include in your letter to yourself.

- Now that you're in this "better" place, how would you describe the Self that is going to need to read this letter later? In other words, who is the Self that you are writing this letter to? For example, is this a letter to Your Unwell Self, Your Depressed Self, Your Avoiding Self, Your Self-Harming Self?
- What does that future You need to know? For example, some people struggle to remember when they are in a depressive episode that they haven't always felt that way. Are there words of reassurance or encouragement that you want your future Self to hear?
- Are there specific skills that you know are helpful for you when you get into that painful state? What do you want that future You to know, or to remember? For example, some people like to remind themselves to practice a certain mindfulness exercise; others find writing out self-validating statements when they start to experience familiar painful emotions such as shame quite helpful. But

this can also include reminders like "get fresh air every day" or "exercise really helps our mood!"
- Is there anything else you'd like to share with your future Self?

When you're ready, you can put this information into a letter to yourself. Some people find it helpful to think of this as an instruction manual for themselves! The key is, once you've created this letter or instruction manual, to make sure you keep it somewhere you'll remember to look at it when you start to struggle with tolerating distressing emotions. You might make it part of your routine to read your letter once a week, or put a reminder in your phone so you remember to look at it. Or you might keep it on your dresser or night table so you see it every day. You'll also probably want to add new things that you find helpful over time.

Your next step is to continue to practice what you've learned. Using these skills when things get difficult will of course be helpful, and you'll likely find it even more helpful to practice when you're not in a full-blown crisis; over time you'll likely see that you experience fewer crises as your ability to tolerate distress increases. Remember that learning to tolerate distress and manage emotions is a process, so do your best to have patience and be gentle with yourself. Radically accept when you struggle—none of us is perfect—and keep working to change.

REFERENCES

Anderson, W.P., C.M. Reid, and G.L. Jennings. 1992. "Pet Ownership and Risk Factors for Cardiovascular Disease." *Medical Journal of Australia* 157(5): 298–301.

Babyak, M., J.A. Blumenthal, S. Herman, P. Khatri, M. Doraiswamy, K. Moore, W. Edward Craighead, T.T. Baldewicz, and K. Ranga Krishnan. 2000. "Exercise Treatment for Major Depression: Maintenance of Therapeutic Benefit at 10 Months." *Psychosomatic Medicine* 62(5): 633–8.

Beil, K., and D. Hanes. 2013. "The Influence of Urban Natural and Built Environments on Physiological and Psychological Measures of Stress—A Pilot Study." *International Journal of Environmental Research and Public Health* 10(4): 1250–67.

Bernstein, E.E., and R.J. McNally. 2017. "Acute Aerobic Exercise Helps Overcome Emotion Regulation Deficits." *Cognition and Emotion* 31(4): 834–43.

Dolgoff-Kaspar, R., A. Baldwin, M.S. Johnson, N. Edling, and G.K. Sethi. 2012. "Effect of Laughter Yoga on Mood and Heart Rate Variability in Patients Awaiting Organ Transplantation: A Pilot Study." *Alternative Therapies in Health and Medicine* 18(5): 61–6.

Ekman, P., and R.J. Davidson. 1993. "Voluntary Smiling Changes Regional Brain Activity." *Psychological Science* 4(5): 342–45.

Frostadottir, A.D., and D. Dorjee. 2019. "Effects of Mindfulness Based Cognitive Therapy (MBCT) and Compassion Focused Therapy (CFT) on Symptom Change, Mindfulness, Self-Compassion, and Rumination in Clients with Depression, Anxiety, and Stress." *Frontiers in Psychology* 10: 1099.

Germer, C. 2009. *The Mindful Path to Self-Compassion: Freeing Yourself from Destructive Thoughts and Emotions*. New York: Guilford Press.

Germer, C., and K. Neff. n.d. "Soften, Soothe, Allow : Working with Emotions in the Body." Meditation. https://selfcompassion.org/category/exercises/#guided-meditations.

Greenwood, K.A., R. Thurston, M. Rumble, S.J. Waters, and F.J. Keefe. 2003. "Anger and Persistent Pain: Current Status and Future Directions." *Pain* 103(1–2): 1–5.

Kerns, R.D., R. Rosenberg, and M.C. Jacob. 1994. "Anger Expression and Chronic Pain." *Journal of Behavioral Medicine* 17(1): 57–67.

Linehan, M.M. 1993. *Cognitive-Behavioral Treatment of Borderline Personality Disorder*. New York: Guilford Press.

Linehan, M.M. 2005. *Crisis Survival Skills: Part One—Distracting and Self-Soothing*. DVD. Seattle: Dawkins Productions/Behavioral Tech.

Linehan, M.M. 2014. *DBT Skills Training Manual*. 2nd ed. New York: Guilford Press.

Serpell, J. 1991. "Beneficial Effects of Pet Ownership on Some Aspects of Human Health and Behaviour." *Journal of the Royal Society of Medicine* 84(12): 717–20.

Siegel, D. 2014. *Brainstorm: The Power and Purpose of the Teenage Brain*. New York: Jeremy P. Tarcher/Penguin.

Van Dijk, S. 2012. *Calming the Emotional Storm: Using Dialectical Behavior Therapy Skills to Manage Your Emotions and Balance Your Life*. Oakland, CA: New Harbinger Publications.

Van Dijk, S. 2013. *DBT Made Simple: A Step-by-Step Guide to Dialectical Behavior Therapy*. Oakland, CA: New Harbinger Publications.

Zimmer, C. 2021. "Scientists Finish the Human Genome at Last." The New York Times, July 23. https://www.nytimes.com/2021/07/23/science/human-genome-complete.html.

Sheri Van Dijk, MSW, is a psychotherapist, and renowned dialectical behavior therapy (DBT) expert. She is author of several books, including *Calming the Emotional Storm, Don't Let Your Emotions Run Your Life for Teens,* and *The DBT Skills Workbook for Teen Self-Harm.* Her books focus on using DBT skills to help people manage their emotions and cultivate lasting well-being. She is also the recipient of the R.O. Jones Award from the Canadian Psychiatric Association.

Matthew McKay, PhD, is a professor at the Wright Institute in Berkeley, CA. He has authored and coauthored numerous books, including *Self-Esteem, Thoughts and Feelings, When Anger Hurts,* and *ACT on Life Not on Anger.* McKay received his PhD in clinical psychology from the California School of Professional Psychology, and specializes in the cognitive behavioral treatment of anxiety and depression. He lives and works in the Greater San Francisco Bay Area.

Jeffrey C. Wood, PsyD, lives and works in Las Vegas, NV. He specializes in brief therapy treatments for depression, anxiety, and trauma. He also provides coaching for spiritual development, communication skills development, and life skills. Wood is coauthor of *The New Happiness, The Dialectical Behavior Therapy Skills Workbook,* and *The Dialectical Behavior Therapy Diary.*

Jeffrey Brantley, MD, is professor emeritus in the department of psychiatry and human behavior at Duke University Medical Center. He is founder and former director of the Mindfulness Based Stress Reduction (MBSR) Program at Duke Integrative Medicine. He has represented the Duke MBSR program in numerous radio, television, and print interviews. He is author of *Calming Your Anxious Mind*, and coauthor of the *Five Good Minutes* series.

Patrick Fanning is a professional writer in the mental health field, and founder of a men's support group in Northern California. He has authored and coauthored twelve self-help books, including *Self-Esteem*, *Thoughts and Feelings*, *Couple Skills*, and *Mind and Emotions*.

Erica Pool, PsyD, earned her doctorate at the Wright Institute in Berkeley, CA; and has clinical and research experience at the University of California, Berkeley; and the VA Northern California Health Care System; and has consulted with mental health start-ups. The goal of her work is to understand processes at the core of human suffering to help craft individualized and culturally responsive treatments.

Patricia E. Zurita Ona, PsyD, "Dr. Z," is a psychologist specializing in working with and creating compassionate, research-based, and actionable resources for overachievers and overthinkers to get them unstuck from worries, fears, anxieties, perfectionism, procrastination, obsessions, and ineffective "playing it safe" actions. She is founder of the East Bay Behavior Therapy Center—a boutique practice where she offers therapy and coaching services based on acceptance and commitment therapy (ACT) and contextual behavioral science (CBS). She has been nominated as a fellow of the Association of Contextual Behavioral Science for her contributions to the applications of ACT to specific fear-based struggles.

Real change is possible

For more than forty-five years, New Harbinger has published proven-effective self-help books and pioneering workbooks to help readers of all ages and backgrounds improve mental health and well-being, and achieve lasting personal growth. In addition, our spirituality books offer profound guidance for deepening awareness and cultivating healing, self-discovery, and fulfillment.

Founded by psychologist Matthew McKay and Patrick Fanning, New Harbinger is proud to be an independent, employee-owned company. Our books reflect our core values of integrity, innovation, commitment, sustainability, compassion, and trust. Written by leaders in the field and recommended by therapists worldwide, New Harbinger books are practical, accessible, and provide real tools for real change.

MORE BOOKS from
NEW HARBINGER PUBLICATIONS

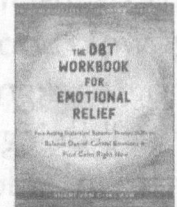

THE DBT WORKBOOK FOR EMOTIONAL RELIEF
Fast-Acting Dialectical Behavior Therapy Skills to Balance Out-of-Control Emotions and Find Calm Right Now

THE DBT SKILLS DAILY JOURNAL
10 Minutes a Day to Soothe Your Emotions with Dialectical Behavior Therapy

SIMPLE WAYS TO UNWIND WITHOUT ALCOHOL
50 Tips to Drink Less and Enjoy More

THE SUICIDAL THOUGHTS WORKBOOK
CBT Skills to Reduce Emotional Pain, Increase Hope, and Prevent Suicide

DBT SKILLS FOR HIGHLY SENSITIVE PEOPLE
Make Emotional Sensitivity Your Superpower Using Dialectical Behavior Therapy

THE ANXIETY FIRST AID KIT
Quick Tools for Extreme, Uncertain Times

newharbingerpublications
1-800-748-6273 / newharbinger.com
(VISA, MC, AMEX / prices subject to change without notice)   Follow Us

Subscribe to our email list at **newharbinger.com/subscribe**

BACK COVER MATERIAL

STAY GROUNDED—NO MATTER WHAT LIFE THROWS YOUR WAY

Let's face it: Life can feel downright overwhelming at times, and struggles can arise when you least expect them. Whether it's a bad breakup or divorce, illness, loss of a job, or even a natural disaster or pandemic, sometimes you need a little extra help managing difficult emotions when times get tough. This go-to guide is packed with proven-effective skills you can use anytime, anywhere to keep cool and thrive in the face of life's inevitable challenges.

Grounded in evidence-based dialectical behavior therapy (DBT), **Distress Tolerance Made Easy** offers essential tools for staying grounded, no matter what. You'll learn to navigate difficult experiences and setbacks—without resorting to unhealthy coping habits. And as you practice and hone the skills outlined in this guide, you'll discover you *can* handle whatever life throws your way—without avoidance, anger, or despair. Life happens, but you don't have to get pulled under. Grab this book and head for calmer waters.

"A much-needed, valuable guide to making sense of distress—and responding more effectively to it."

—Joel Minden, PhD, author of *Show Your Anxiety Who's Boss*

www.ingramcontent.com/pod-product-compliance
Lightning Source LLC
Chambersburg PA
CBHW011944150426
43192CB00017B/2780